Webster's

Household & Home Repair Dictionary

® Landoll, Inc.
© 1997 Landoll, Inc.
Ashland, Ohio 44805

INTRODUCTION

This HOUSEHOLD & HOME REPAIR DICTIONARY is designed to be of help to anyone who has a home, whether you own it or rent it and whether it's a house or an apartment. It covers not just the usual stain removal or cooking substitution subjects, but also minor repairs to furniture, cars and other household items, and "how to" instructions to perform certain jobs for we who have had little or no training in such matters.

Every item has been categorized as much as possible to make it easy for you to find, and then put into alphabetical order to simplify things even more. In addition, there is sometimes more than one way to do something, which I have included if possible.

Diagrams have been added to help explain how to do the job or to show you what the result will be.

I hope you will find this dictionary valuable and I hope that the results will be as good for you as they have been for me!

Janis Hawkridge
Compiler & Editor

CONTENTS

BATHROOMS

BATHTUBS, ENAMEL, WHITENING OF
Rub the enamel with a solution of salt and turpentine.

BATHTUB STAINS
Chlorine will usually remove bathtub and sink stains.

Or mix 3 tablespoons of cream of tartar and 1 tablespoon of hydrogen peroxide to a thin paste and wipe on with a cloth. Kerosene is also a good cleaning agent.

For brown iron stains, rub with a cut lemon dipped in salt.

CHROME, CLEANING
To polish chrome, use dry baking soda on a soft cloth.

CHROME, RUSTY
To remove rust spots, rub them with aluminum foil and then wipe with a dry cloth.

COMBS & BRUSHES, CLEANING

To clean and sterilize combs and hairbrushes, add 3 cups of sudsy ammonia to 1 cup of water and soak them for half an hour. Rinse well in cold water.

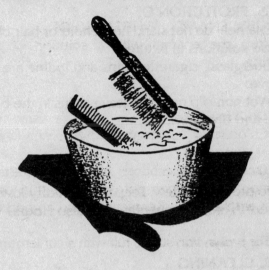

DENTURES, CLEANING

To clean and sterilize dentures, ordinary household bleach does an excellent job. Put dentures in a container, cover with water and add 2 tablespoons of bleach. Soak for 15 minutes and then rinse with water.

DRAIN PROTECTION

If you wash your hair in the shower, place a piece of steel wool over the drain. This will trap any loose hair that might clog the plumbing. It's also handy when you wash the dog or cat.

FITTINGS, PROTECTION OF

Enamel: do not stand household or hair bleach or other acid solutions in fixtures.

Fiberglass: cigarette burns and iodine are difficult to remove.

Wet non-slip mats can leave stains in the bath tub. Remove and dry them.

MILDEW

To prevent mildew, keep the humidity low and air out closed-in areas frequently. See also Floors.

MIRROR, CLEANING

To remove hair spray, wipe with methylated spirits.

MOUTHWASH

Gargle with mixture of 1 teaspoon of baking soda in a half glass of warm water.

SHOWER CAP

When your shower cap tears or rips just as you are

trying to put it on, and you have no spare, use a plastic bag from the kitchen, twist the corner to make it tight around your head, and fasten with a hair clip.

SHOWER NOZZLE, CLOGGED

If the spray nozzle in your bathroom shower has become clogged because of hard water, immerse it in vinegar and soak it overnight.

Or boil it in a half-cup of vinegar and a quart of water for 15 minutes.

SOAP DISHES

If you are tired of washing the gooey soap dishes in the bathroom, get a soap or hand-lotion dispenser. Fill it with liquid soap, dishwashing detergent or shampoo. It's neat, easy to use and to clean.

SPONGES, CLEANING

When synthetic sponges get dirty and smell bad, put them in cold water with a little vinegar and salt added and let them soak for a few hours.

STEAM

To quickly clear up steam in the bathroom, turn the cold water on full force.

Or fill the bathtub with 2 inches of cold water

before running the hot water to avoid steaming up the bathroom.

TILE, DISCOLORED

If the grouting between the tiles becomes discolored, clean it with a solution of household bleach or liquid antiseptic on a toothbrush.

TILE, MILDEWED

If the grout between the tiles on your bathroom walls become mildewed, the easiest solution is to paint the grout and the caulking around the tub with some liquid porcelain repair. It comes in a bottle with a small brush that makes it easy to apply.

WALLS, CLEANING OF

To clean bathroom walls, run the hot water in the tub or shower, and close the door until the room is steamy. This makes the walls easier to clean.

WATER, HARD

To remove hard water stains on tiles and shower glass, apply neat vinegar, leave it on for 10 minutes, and rinse off.

CLOSETS

BELT HANGER

A simple and effective belt hanger, which can help you to keep matching belts with your suit or skirt, can be made with a piece of cardboard with holes cut out to loop the belt through.

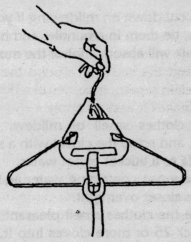

CEDAR

Cedar will protect your clothes from moths. To turn your closet into a cedar lined one, nail the pieces of cedar right over the walls.

To refresh an old cedar closet or chest, give the boards a sanding.

Or paint your closet with cedar oil (obtainable at the hardware store).

COAT HOOKS

Impale small sponge-rubber balls on the coat hooks to prevent damaging the clothes.

DAMP

You can cut down on mildewing if you take 6-12 pieces of chalk, tie them in a bundle, and hang them in the closet. Chalk will absorb a lot of the moisture.

DEODORIZING

If your clothes smell of mildew, hang them outdoors to air, and scrub the closet with a solution of 1 cup baking soda to a bucket of hot water.

Or place a pan containing water and household ammonia in the closet overnight.

To make the clothes smell pleasant, take a firm orange and stick 25 or more cloves into it. Put it in a warm, dry place to dry slowly and thoroughly. As the rind shrinks the cloves will be gripped more firmly. Hang it in the closet to give a good aroma.

DOORLESS

Try using a venetian blind of the proper width if

you have a closet without a door. It also helps provide good ventilation to your clothes.

GARMENT BAGS

Use old pillow cases as garment bags by cutting a hole in the center of the seamed end.

HANGERS

To avoid or get rid of an unwanted crease in pants, cut a cardboard mailing tube to fit the bottom wire of the hanger. Slit it full-length and slip it over the wire.

Or do the same thing with several thicknesses of newspaper, held on with adhesive tape.

HANGER, FALLING

To prevent coat hangers from falling off closet rods, wind a large rubber band several times around the end of the hoot, to act as a brake.

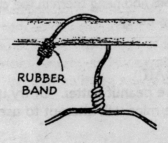

RUBBER
BAND

HANGER ROD

Instead of using a rod, try using a piece of chain to put the hangers on. Hangers hook into the links, so the clothes don't get pushed together and wrinkled.

MOTH PREVENTION

Hang mothballs, etc., as high as possible in your clothes closets. The fumes filter downwards.

MOTH REMOVAL

To remove moths from a closet or a bag, fill an old sock with moth crystals and attach it by a rubber band to the hose of your hairdryer. Put the dryer on its "cold" setting, place it on a closet shelf and close the door, or in the garment bag, and let it run for 10-15 minutes.

MOTH REPELLENT

Wrap lemon peel in a piece of cheesecloth or other porous cloth and hang them in the closet. The odor keeps the moths away.

MOUSETRAP BAIT

Mice love peanut butter. Or try using absorbent cotton, and the mice will attempt to use it as lining for their nests.

NEATENING

Place rubber-headed tacks about two inches apart on top of the wooden clothes rod to keep the hangers from bunching up.

SHELF PAPER

Slightly dampen the shelves with a sponge before placing the paper. This will give just the right amount of adhesion before you replace articles on the shelves.

Or coat the shelf with wax before laying the paper.

SILENCER

Sliding the clothes hangers along a metal or wooden pole can be disturbing. To allow the hangers to glide noiselessly and also protect the finish on the pole, cover it with ribbed polyethylene plastic and tape the joint. Hangers will slide easily and quietly.

Or coat the rod with paste wax and then polish it.

SILVERFISH EXTERMINATION

Silverfish feed on starch, found in book-bindings, wallpaper glue and starched clothing. Apply a little cinnamon spice in the corners of drawers and closets to discourage them.

WARPED DOORS

If your closet door is warped, apply heat from an ordinary heat lamp to the convex side. Do not hold the lamp too close, as it may damage the finish. Remove the heat as soon as the warp disappears. Coat both sides and edges with sealer to prevent further warping.

COOKING & FOOD

APPLES, CRANBERRY

Remove the core and fill the cavity with cranberry sauce, then bake. Makes a good complement to roast pork.

APPLE SAUCE

Make your apple sauce at the same time as your roast. Put apple, sugar and spices into a separate, covered casserole, and bake. This also improves the flavor.

BABY FOOD, HEATING

A quick and easy way to heat up baby food is to place the required amount in a egg poacher filled with hot water. Put the lid on, and food will heat enough quickly.

BACON, SEPARATING

When bacon strips get stuck together in the package, roll the package gently between your hands before opening.

BAKING

To grease baking pans, slip a plastic sandwich bag over your hand, take a pinch of shortening and rub over the pan.

BAKING POWDER SUBSTITUTE

Mix 1 teaspoon of baking soda with 2 teaspoons cream of tartar.

BATTER, MIXING

Add the salt to the flour before wetting it to prevent lumps.

Or pour flour into the liquid, instead of liquid into the flour, and beat with a fork. This will also prevent lumps.

BREAD, BAKING

When baking bread or rolls, if the oven is too hot and the loaves brown on top before the bread itself is baked, place a pan of boiling water on the top grate. The steam will prevent the bread from scorching while the loaf finishes baking.

To make the top of the loaf shiny, rub it with vinegar when almost baked, then return it to the oven for a few minutes.

Or coat the top of the loaf with egg white. Add sugar for a sweeter flavor.

BREAD, LEFTOVER

Use leftover slices to make bread sticks, croutons, breadcrumbs, or add to meat loaf or puddings.

BREAD STUFFING

Bread used for stuffing poultry will grate easier and quicker if you freeze the bread first.

BURNING FOOD

If you burn potatoes, rice, chili or beans in a pot, you can save most of it by removing the lid and placing the pot in cold water. All the ingredients that do not cling to the bottom can be removed and the burned taste will be gone.

Or, take what is still good and place it in another pan. Cover with a clean, damp cloth and let stand for a while. This should eliminate the smoky taste.

BUTTER, HOMEMADE WHIPPED

Mix 1 pound of homemade butter with 1 pound of margarine. Wash and whip. This has more vitamins and few calories than plain butter.

CAKES, NON-STICK

After you take the cake from the oven, place it on a cloth wrung out in cold water for a few minutes. The cake will then turn out of the baking pan easily.

CAKES, DRIED FRUIT IN
To prevent the raisins or other dried fruit from falling to the bottom of the batter, first pour hot water over them and let them stand for a few minutes. Drain, and mix them with the flour used in the cake.

CAKES, FILLING
To prevent the cake filling from soaking into the cake, sprinkle the top of each layer with powdered sugar before frosting or filling.

CAKES, STICKING
Hold the cake pan over a low flame for 5-8 seconds. The cake should come out perfectly.

CAULIFLOWER, TO PREVENT DISCOLORATION OF
Add a teaspoon of lemon juice to the water while cooking.

CELERY CLEANING
To clean celery, use a piece of hacksaw blade. The teeth will reach into the grooves of the celery. A short piece of broomstick, or several wraps of tape around one

end, will make a good handle.

CELERY, CRISP

Immerse the celery in cold water with a couple of ice cubes for a few minutes before serving.

CEREAL, BREAKFAST

Try grating lemon or orange zest onto the cereal (hot or cold) to create a different taste.

CHEESE, TO GRATE

Chilled cheese grates more easily than room temperature cheese.

If you need only a small amount of grated cheese, use the vegetable peeler.

CHEESE, OLD

Hard, old cheese can be grated and used sprinkled on top of vegetables, sauces and soups.

CHICKEN, TO TENDERIZE

Rub the inside and outside of the chicken with lemon juice after cleaning and before adding dressing.

When boiling a chicken, add a teaspoon of lemon juice or vinegar to the water to tenderize.

CHOCOLATE, MELTING

To keep it from sticking to the pan when melting it for cake filling, rub the inside of the pan with a little butter or olive oil.

COCONUT

To freshen shredded coconut, soak in fresh milk to which you've added a dash of sugar. Let it soak for several minutes before using.

Or place coconut in a sieve over boiling water, and steam it until moist.

COFFEE, GRINDING

When grinding fresh coffee, add a piece of cinnamon stick for a spicy touch.

COFFEE, ICED

Don't throw away leftover coffee. Pour it into ice cube trays, freeze and store in a plastic freezer bag. To make iced coffee, simply put a few cubes into a glass and allow to partially melt. No need for ice, which would dilute the drink.

COFFEE, TO KEEP HOT AND FRESH

Put fresh hot coffee in a thermos to keep the flavor fresh for later.

COOKIES

Chill the cookie dough before shaping and baking it for greater ease of handling. If you're rushed for time, 20 minutes in the freezer equals 2 hours in the refrigerator.

CORNED BEEF

Make it more tender by mixing a teaspoon of vinegar with the cooking water. Add a clove of garlic and a bay leaf to improve flavor.

CROUTONS

Croutons can be made easily in a corn popper. Cut the bread into the desired size, place in the popper. They will crisp very quickly.

DOUGHNUTS

When frying them, add a few whole cloves to the fat to improve the flavor.

DOUGHNUTS, STALE

Split them and dip in French toast batter (1 egg to half-cup of milk), and brown quickly in butter or margarine.

DRESSING, SALAD

Mix a quarter cup peanut oil with 1 tablespoon of vinegar. Add a half teaspoon of salt, freshly ground pepper to taste and a little crushed garlic.

DRESSING, SALAD, FRENCH

Brush French dressing over meat and vegetables while broiling them to add flavor and aid browning.

DRESSING, SALAD, LO-CAL

Mix 2 thirds of a cup of cottage cheese, 1 third of a cup fresh grapefruit juice, 2 tablespoons fresh lemon or lime juice, 1 teaspoon grated lemon rind, half a teaspoon of salt and 1 eighth of a teaspoon each of ground black pepper and paprika. Beat with an electric or rotary beater.

DRESSING, SALAD, RUSSIAN

Add chili sauce and diced pimento to mayonnaise or creamy salad dressing.

EGGS, BOILING

If the eggs crack while boiling, spray them lavishly with salt and this will seal the cracks.

EGGS, HARD-BOILED

If the hard-boiled eggs are to be served cold, place them in cold water as soon as they are cooked. This prevents the outsides of the yolks from turning dark, and makes the eggs easier to peel. Make sure the eggs are cold before peeling.

EGGS, OMELETTE

Add a half teaspoon of baking powder to every 4 eggs. After beating the eggs thoroughly the omelette will be lighter, fluffier and tastier.

Try cooking it in a double boiler instead of a pan. It will come out fluffy and moist.

Omelettes won't collapse if you add a pinch of cornstarch and a pinch of powdered sugar to each egg before it is beaten.

EGGS, POACHED

Put a piece of waxed paper in the bottom of the pan to prevent the eggs from sticking.

To keep the egg whites fluffy and not flat, add 1 teaspoon of vinegar to the water.

EGGS, SCRAMBLED

Sprinkle Parmesan cheese on scrambled eggs while you are cooking them.

20

EGGS, SLICING HARD BOILED

Slice hardboiled eggs with a piece of ordinary sewing thread.

Or, if you use a knife, dip it in boiling water first to prevent the yolks from crumbling.

EGGS, SUBSTITUTE FOR

One teaspoon of cornstarch for each egg required makes a good substitute when cooking cakes.

FISH, SCALING

Place the fish in a large can, pour boiling water over it, and remove quickly. Immediately drop into cold water.

To scale fish, use a round steel pot cleaner instead of a knife.

Sometimes, rubbing vinegar over the fish beforehand makes scaling easier.

FRUIT, DRIED

Stale raisins and other dried fruit can be freshened by putting them in a strainer and setting it over a pot of boiling water, covered, for about 15 minutes.

FRUIT, TO KEEP FRESH

After slicing pears, apples and bananas for fruit

salads, etc., dip them in lemon juice to prevent discoloration.

Dip peach slices in milk to keep them fresh.

FRUIT, PREPARATION

Browning: sprinkle peeled fruit with lemon juice, or peel fruit into a bowl of salted water. Rinse the salt off before use.

Citrus: grapefruits, lemons, limes and oranges will give you more juice if you warm them in a bowl of hot water for 15 minutes before squeezing.

To remove peel and pith more easily, pop oranges into a hot oven (200C, 400F) for a few minutes.

Lemons: To save wasting a whole lemon when you need just a little juice for a recipe, make a little hole in the lemon with a toothpick and squeeze out only the required amount of juice. Use the toothpick as a plug after, wrap the lemon in foil and put in the refrigerator.

Always grate the lemon before you squeeze it. Dip the grater in cold water so the grated peel slips off more easily.

Peeling: for grapes, peaches, pears and tomatoes, put the fruit in a bowl and pour boiling water over them. Leave for a few minutes, drain and cover with cold water. When cool, peel.

Strawberries: wash them before you remove the stalk, so they won't go soggy.

FUDGE

To improve flavor and texture to homemade fudge, add a teaspoon of cornstarch.

Or after mixing all ingredients together, let the mixture stand for a while before cooking. The sugar will dissolve, and the fudge will have a much better texture.

GARLIC

Spear the garlic clove with a toothpick so it's easy to find and remove from the sauce or soup.

GINGER ROOT

To keep ginger root fresh, bury it in a pot in the garden until needed, then re-bury it.

GRAVY, CREAMY

Creamy gravy or sauces can be made more quickly and smoother if the flour and water thickening is prepared ahead of time. Put water in a fruit jar, drop the flour in, cover the jar and shake until the paste is smooth.

GRAVY, LUMPY

Always add liquid slowly to prevent lumps, and stir and scrape with a spoon. If there are lumps, strain the gravy through a sieve and reheat.

GREEN ONIONS & SHALLOTS

Green onions and shallots will stay fresh longer if you place the bunch in a plant pot in the garden and keep them damp.

GREASE SPLATTER

To prevent grease from splattering out of the pan, sprinkle it with a little salt or flour before you add the grease.

Or, after grease is added, turn a colander upside down over the pan. It will stop the grease splattering but still allow air in.

HERBS, DRYING

To dry fresh herbs, tie in loose bundles and hang them upside down inside a paper bag. When dry, run a rolling pin over the bag, or rub them between your fingers to crush them and remove the stalks without mess. Store in china or dark glass jars with well-fitting lids. Dried herbs are four times as strong as herbs used fresh.

HERBS, FREEZING

Freeze whole in foil or plastic bags. Once frozen they will crumble easily. Herbs are stronger dried or frozen than they are if they are used fresh.

ICE CUBES

To prevent ice cubes from sticking together, spray them with soda water.

JAMS & JELLIES, HOMEMADE

Add a teaspoon of glycerin to each pint of jam or jelly. This will prevent it from crystallizing, and you will need less sugar.

Before pouring hot paraffin on the jelly or other preserve, coil a piece of string over the top of the jam and let it hang over the edge of the jar. This makes it easier to remove the paraffin later.

STRING

LEMONS, HARD

Cover hard lemons with boiling water and let them stand for a few minutes.

LETTUCE

Keep lettuce fresh for days by washing it thoroughly, separating the leaves and putting them into a tin with an airtight cover.

MEATBALLS, PREPARATION

To prepare them with less mess, lightly oil your hands so the mixture won't stick, shape them and place on a lightly greased cookie sheet. Bake at 350 degrees for 15 minutes.

For Swedish or hors d'oeuvres-type meatballs, use a melon baller to shape them

MEAT LOAF

Fill muffin tins with the meat loaf mixture, rather than making one large one. Individual loaves are fun to eat, especially for children.

To prevent meat loaf from sticking to the pan, lay a strip of raw bacon in the pan before adding the unbaked mixture.

MEAT LOAF EXTENDER

To extend the meat loaf, add: bread crumbs or cubes, cracker crumbs, brown or white rice, dry oatmeal, bulgar wheat, barley, finely grated carrots, potatoes or zucchini.

MILK, SOUR

Add 2 tablespoons of lemon juice to 1 cup of milk to sour it for recipes.

NUTS, BLANCHING

Nuts are blanched by immersing them in boiling water for 2 minutes, then putting them into cold water. Drain, and remove the skins, spread thinly in an oven-proof pan and put in a warm oven to dry for a few hours. The crispness will depend upon their dryness.

OIL, CLARIFYING

Line a funnel with paper towel or a paper coffee filter. Pour the oil back into your storage container through the paper and funnel.

ONION

If your eyes water when peeling onions, try wearing a pair of swim goggles.

To remove the odor from your hands and the cutting board, rub with fresh lemon.

ORANGES, SWEET

Choose the navel oranges with the largest navels if you want the sweetest ones.

PANCAKES

To make attractive and delicious pancakes: turn them only once. Cook until the cakes are covered with bubbles and the edges look dry, then turn and cook the other side. Serve them straight off the griddle - stacking them and letting them stand can make them soggy.

PANCAKES, SYRUP FOR

If you're out of syrup, try mixing a little water and some butter with a little jelly, and heating it up. Makes a delicious fruit syrup.

PASTA, TO COOK

To prevent pasta or noodles from sticking together, add several drops of oil to the water before cooking.

When water forms on a plate of pasta, it's because the pasta was steaming when dished up, turning to water. To prevent this, gently toss the pasta till it stops steaming before serving.

PIE CRUST

To improve the flavor and texture of pie crust, add a little sugar to each cup of flour used in making the crust.

Or add a pinch of spice or herb: apple or pumpkin pie - cinnamon, or nutmeg; mincemeat pie - clove; meat pie - sage or caraway seed.

PIE CRUST, BAKING
If your pie shell bubbles or shrinks during baking, try baking them between to pie tins of the same size, and of light weight, such as tin or aluminum. After 10 minutes in the oven, remove the top tin and continue baking until brown.

PIE, FRUIT
Bake the pie shell for about 5 minutes before putting in the fruit. This will stop the lower crust from becoming soggy.

PIE, MEAT
To prevent the gravy soaking through the lower crust, brush egg white over the crust.

PIE, MERINGUE
To cut a meringue-topped pie without the meringue sticking to the knife, dip the knife in milk first.

POTATO, BAKED
Speed up the baking by soaking the potato in hot water for 10-15 minutes.

29

POTATO, BOILED

When boiling, add a little milk to the water and the potatoes will not darken as they boil.

POTATO, MASHED

Just before mashing, add a teaspoon of baking powder. Beat vigorously, and they will turn out light and creamy.

POTATO SALAD

If you like onion flavor but not onion, boil a peeled onion with the unpeeled potatoes. The onion flavor will be absorbed.

ROAST, BURNED

Soak a towel in hot water, wring out well and place over the meat. Leave it for 5 minutes, then scrape off burned parts.

SALT

When you add the salt in your cooking is important. With soups and sauces, put it in early. With meats, add it just before taking them from the stove. For cakes, mix the salt with the eggs. Salt the water the vegetables cook in, and put the salt in the frying pan before frying fish.

SALT, OVERSALTING

If gravy or soup is over salty, put in a few pieces of toasted bread for a few minutes and then remove them. They will absorb a lot of the salt.

SOUP, CANNED

Before opening the can, shake it well. This mixes the ingredients in the soup, and then, when you add the water, there won't be any lumps, especially in creamed soups.

SOUP, VEGETABLE

Add a few cloves to the soup to improve flavor.

SPAGHETTI, TO COOK

See Pasta.

SPAGHETTI SAUCE

To get rid of oil that accumulates on the top of the sauce, stir in the juice of half a lemon and 1 tablespoon of granulated sugar.

SPICES

Put bay leaves, peppercorns, garlic, etc., in a tea caddy and hang them into the pot while cooking. This will flavor the food without being difficult to remove.

SUGAR, BROWN

To keep it soft and fresh, remove it from the box and place in a plastic bag without holes. Seal well.

VEGETABLES, FROZEN

To thaw them faster, place them, package as well, in cold water.

Most vegetables can be cooked from frozen, except corn on the cob and spinach.

VEGETABLES, TO KEEP FRESH

Squeeze lemon juice on the cut surfaces after preparing vegetables.

VINEGAR

For cooking, and for rinsing hair, apple cider vinegar has a better smell.

WINE, CHILLING

A bottle of wine can be chilled quickly if you place it in a piece of flannel that has been dipped in cold water and not wrung out. This will usually bring the wine below room temperature quickly.

YEAST

When yeast is used, put it into a little warm water, add a teaspoon of sugar, and let it develop a while before adding it to the dough mixture. This will make the dough rise more quickly and easily, and give your bread a better texture.

ELECTRICAL & PLUMBING

AIR CONDITIONER

Periodic cleaning and replacement of filters can save up to 10% on your cooling costs.

APPLIANCES

Your oven, furnace, refrigerator, water heater, air conditioner and clothes dryer account for three quarters of the energy you use in your home.

Keep all instruction books together in a safe place, and re-read them periodically. If one gets lost, write to the manufacturer for a replacement.

APPLIANCE FAILURE

Unplug the appliance and check the socket by plugging in another appliance. If the socket doesn't work, check the main fuse box. If the appliance is not working, check the fuse and connections inside the plug.

CISTERN OVERFLOW

IF your cistern is overflowing, stop more water entering it by removing the cistern top and tying the lever arm to a piece of wood placed across the top of the cistern.

DRAIN CARE

To prevent clogging, keep the drains clean and free of grease accumulations and disagreeable odors by rinsing them with strong hot salt water at least once each week.

DRAIN, CLOGGED BATHTUB

First, try to move the waste material by chemical solvents. If these fail, try a plunger: remove the attachment in the tub that turns on the shower extension. Stick a wet cloth or wash rag into the hole so no air leaks through. Then place the plunger over the drain and agitate it vigorously up and down. If this doesn't work, use an auger (snake).

DRAINPIPES, CLOGGED

Use a plunger to suck out the refuse. Hold the plunger cup over the drain, cover it with 3-4 inches of water, and pump the handle up and down vigorously. If the plunger doesn't work, use a plumbing solvent, available at hardware stores and some supermarkets. If both these methods fail, examine the fixture for a trap below (a loop in the pipe). Place a bucket below the trap, and remove the connections holding the trap with a pipe wrench. Clean the trap with a wire or auger (snake), scour it with hot, soapy water and replace the trap. Tighten firmly.

Grease and soap clinging to a pipe can sometimes be removed by flushing with hot water. Lye or lye mixed with a small amount of aluminum shavings may also be used. When cold water is added, the violent gas-forming reaction and production of heat that takes place loosens the grease and soap and they are flushed away. Use cold water only.

Do not use chemical cleansers on pipes that are completely stopped up, because they must be brought into direct contact with the stoppage to be effective.

DRAINPIPES, FROZEN

Turn off the main supply valve. Open all the faucets connected to the pipe. Apply heat in some form to the end nearest the fixture.

If you are thawing out waste or drain pipes, start heating them from the end away from the fixtures. You may be able to thaw drainpipes by pouring boiling water into the fixture.

Your electric iron is great for thawing out pipes, because of its concentrated heat.

DRAINPIPES, LEAKING

These can be effectively sealed with a homemade poultice. Wrap layers of cloth and wet plaster around the leaky sections, using some strong cord to tie the "bandage" in place. Let this dry before using the pipe.

Small leaks can often be repaired with a rubber patch and metal clamp or sleeve. This must be considered an emergency repair and should be followed by permanent repair as soon as possible. Or try plastic or rubber tubing, strong enough to withstand the normal water pressure in the pipe. Slip it over the open ends of the pipe and fasten with pipe clamps or several turns of wire.

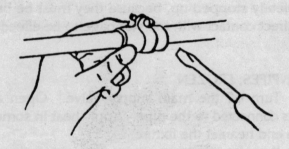

Vibration can sometimes break solder joints in copper tubing, causing leaks. If the joint is accessible, clean and resolder. The tubing must be dry before it can be heated to soldering temperature. If the joint is not accessible, call a plumber.

Large leaks may require cutting out the damaged section of pipe and installing a new piece. At least one union joint will be needed unless the leak is near the end of the pipe.

ELECTRIC BLANKETS

These should be folded end to end, or from side to side, when storing them so the thermostats inside don't get creased. Don't place heavy objects on the blanket, or attempt to pin them. Dry cleaning is not recommended as the solvents can destroy the insulation on the wires. They can be washed.

ELECTRICAL CORDS, STORAGE

Coil the hank of extension cord inside a cardboard tube. The tubes from toilet tissue are the right size for a cord eight feet long.

ELECTRICAL CORDS, MAINTENANCE

Rub a thin coat of wax onto the cord at periodic intervals so the cord doesn't dry out or crack.

ELECTRIC FANS, MAINTENANCE

After you have oiled your electric fan, cover it with a large paper bag and run it at top speed for a few minutes. Then remove the bag. Any excess oil will land on the bag, not in your room.

PAPER BAG

ELECTRICAL EMERGENCY KIT

Keep a kit containing a flashlight with a working battery, a selection of fuses and fuse wires, a screwdriver and candles near the fuse box.

Label all the circuits to make it easier to isolate the one that's not working.

ENERGY CONSERVATION

The total energy used by your blender,

dishwasher, vacuum cleaner, hair dryer and electric toothbrush is less than one third of the energy required for hot water.

FAUCETS, LEAKING

Instead of buying a certain size washer to repair a leaking faucet, cut a washer from a plastic coffee can lid. Cut the plastic carefully and the repair should last for months.

FIREPLACE

Unless you are using your fireplace, keep the damper closed, and save 8% of your heat.

FURNACE

Periodic cleaning and replacement of filters can save you 10% on heating costs.

FUSES

Wind wires clockwise around electric screw terminals in plugs and fuse boxes, so that the action of tightening the screw also tightens the wire.

INSULATION

Insulate your attic to prevent heat loss in the

winter and heat gain in the summer. It can save you up to 30% on your heating and cooling costs.

Use weatherstripping and caulking around doors and windows to reduce heating and cooling costs.

LIGHT BULBS

Install lower wattage and energy-saver bulbs and keep light fixtures clean.

LIGHT BULBS, NOT WORKING

If a new bulb doesn't make contact in the socket, and won't light, instead of putting a tool in the live socket, pry up one edge of the contact plate on the bulb.

PRIED UP

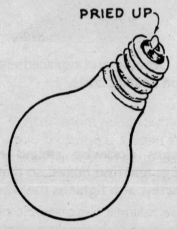

If one light bulb in a multi-bulb fitting fails, change all the other ones at the same time.

LIGHTS, DROPLIGHTS

If the cord on the droplight is too long, and people bang their heads on it, make an "M" shaped clip from a clothes hanger wire and loop the cord through the apexes of the "M" to the desired height. Make sure first that the insulation on the cord is good.

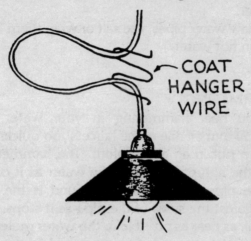

COAT
HANGER
WIRE

OVENS

Dishes that take more than 1 hour to cook generally don't need a pre-heated oven.

If you use glass or ceramic baking dishes you can turn down the heat 20-25 degrees, as they retain heat better.

If you are baking a pie, casserole or roast, turn the oven off 10 minutes before the time is up. This does not apply to cakes.

Putting a lid on the pan, and matching the size of

the pan to the size of the burner, will conserve your electricity or gas.

PIPES, FROZEN
Sprinkle salt down pipes to stop them freezing in cold weather.

To thaw water pipes, use salt or wrap them in rags wrung out in hot water.

PIPES, HAMMERING
If you hear hammering in your water pipes whenever you turn off one of the faucets too quickly, you may have to put in an air cushion. The hammering is caused by the abrupt halting of the water as it courses through the pipes. The banging sound is the water bouncing against the sides of the pipe as it stops.

Install, as near as possible to the water meter, a 3-foot length of pipe capped at the end, and screwed into the main pipe. When the water supply is arrested at the faucet, the water that is stopped will force itself up into the air pocket in the air cushion and will slow down gradually against the compressed air, without knocking in the pipe.

Hammering can also be caused by incorrect support of the pipe at some point along its length. Check the pipe wherever it's exposed in the baseboard to see that all mounting straps are tight. The pipe should be solidly anchored at frequent intervals along its length.

Look for places where the pipe has given or sagged out of line. The vibrations are set up when water rushes rapidly though it.

If the water you receive from the main supply is already pressurized, you may have an unnecessary air pocket in your pipes. Check with your plumber.

PLUMBING

Fat poured down a sink will set fast in the "U" bend. Pour fat instead into an old can and put it in the trash when hardened.

PLUNGER SUBSTITUTE

For sinks, fold a sponge in half, wrapping it around with a dishcloth or flannel and tying it firmly to the end of a rod or wooden spoon. Block the overflows, place the "plunger" over the plug hole and add water to the basin to cover the "plunger". Use a vigorous pumping action.

REPAIRS

Replace the floorboard nails with screws where electricity, gas and water cables or pipes run underneath. It will make it easier for repairs.

SAFETY, ELECTRICAL

Don't run electrical cords where they can become

worn or frayed. Replace worn cords immediately. Keep cords away from heat, water and grease. Never handle cords with wet hands. Even rubber overshoes and gloves are not an absolute guarantee against electrocution. Never use a cord with current-carrying capacity too small for the job. It can overheat, melt the insulation and cause a fire.

Never pull on the cord to get the plug out of the wall socket. It can cause fires.

Never clean or inspect an electrical appliance without turning it off and unplugging it from the power supply.

SAFETY, GAS

If you don't know how to turn off your gas, ask your meter reader next time.

Make sure that, if your gas has been turned off at the mains and then turned on again, all pilot lights are relighted.

Never block flues or ventilators in rooms with gas appliances.

Have gas appliances correctly installed and serviced regularly.

SEPTIC TANKS AND CESSPOOLS

Do not pour fats or oil into either of these, or down the drains. Store instead in old cans and throw out with the garbage. Do not flush heavy paper, rags, coffee grounds or similar down the drain. Do not connect roof gutters, storm drains or other large volume water wastes to the septic tank or cesspool. Separate dry wells should be built for them.

Detergents are frequently fatal to the bacteria needed in a septic tank, but are okay for cesspools. To restart bacterial action in a septic tank, run a quantity of water into any of the plumbing fixtures, dissolve yeast in tepid water, and let the mixture drain out into the tank.

SHORT CIRCUIT

An easy way to find out which appliance blew out is to replace the blown fuse with a 75-700 watt light bulb. The light will shine brightly as long as the short exists. While someone watches the light, quickly unplug each gadget on the circuit. When you hit the defective appliance, the light will dim and you'll know where the repair is needed.

SINK, BLOCKED

Try using a strong solution of washing soda crystals and boiling water.

THERMOSTATS

For energy conservation, set your air conditioner to 76-78 degrees in the summer, and your heater to 66-68 degrees in the winter.

TOILET, NON-FLUSHING

Remove the top of the tank. If the floating hollow ball has a leak, it will not rise when water flows in, so replace the ball. Check the valve washer for wear and replace if necessary. The flush valve is operated by a rubber ball that drops into a hole in the tank bottom when the water has flowed out and seals the hole until the tank refills. If the ball is worn or rotten, replace it.

Sometimes, the wires and arms that hold the float and operate the turn off mechanism become bent or stuck. Twist them straight or free them.

WATER CONSERVATION

Conserve hot water by installing water-saving shower heads. This not only saves water but can reduce your heating bill by 20%.

WATER HEATER

Insulate your water heater with an insulation blanket, and insulate any exposed pipes to minimize heat loss.

Keep the water temperature at 120 degrees, unless you use a dishwasher, in which case set the temperature at 140 degrees.

Indications of overheating are hot water backing up into the cold water supply pipe, or rumbling noises in the hot water tank.

WATER TANK NOISE

Rumbling noises in a hot water tank is a sign of possible overheating which could lead to the development of explosive pressure. Cut off the burner immediately. Be sure the pressure valve is working. Then check the water temperature at the nearest outlet with a thermometer. If it's above what the temperature gauge is set for, check the thermostat that control burner cutoff. If you cannot correct the problem, call a plumber.

EQUIPMENT & TOOLS

ALUMINUM FOIL
Use it to clean chrome and golf clubs, by squeezing some into a ball, dampening it and rubbing over the dirty surface.

BROOM HANDLE
To tighten the handle on a push-broom, wrap the worn threads with heavy cord and then re-insert into the broom head.

BROOM SAVER
Dip the ends of the bristles in a shallow pan of thinned shellac so they don't wear down as fast if you use the broom on rough cement floors or garages.

When the bristles become short and stiff, remove the bottom binding cord and trim the bristles evenly. It will then be reusable for a long time.

CARPET SWEEPER, CLEANING
Remove the brush, take off all hair and lint and rub well with a cloth wetted with kerosene. Wait till odor has evaporated before replacing.

CHAMOIS MAINTENANCE

Wash in lukewarm water and pure soap soapflakes, with a pinch of baking soda. As it tears easily when wet, squeeze it repeatedly to clean it. Do not rub. Rinse in lukewarm water and squeeze out the excess water, or press in a dry towel. Dry in the shade, pulling it gently several times to keep the leather soft.

CLEANING RAG STORAGE

Put the rags used for waxing and polishing into a clean, empty shortening can with a close-fitting lid. It will keep the rags from dirtying your shelves.

CLOCK, NOISY

To silence an electric clock that vibrates from worn bearings, mount it on a quarter-inch pad of foam rubber.

CORD, CUTTING

To cut equal lengths of cord, wrap the string around a suitable width board and cut the cord along the edge of the board with a razor blade.

For cutting quantities of twine or string, a good safe cutter can quickly be made from a window-shade bracket. File the inside edges of the bracket and mount it on the wall or a heavy board with 2 small screws.

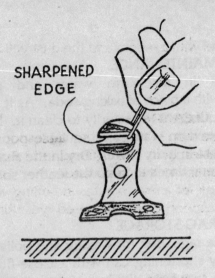

SHARPENED
EDGE

DUSTCLOTHS

Take two sections of paper towel, wet your hands and dry them on the towel. Put a little furniture polish on one of them to polish with, and use the other to buff with.

Or use a soft cloth over a stiff brush for hard-to-reach places.

DUSTCLOTHS, HOMEMADE

Soak pieces of flannel in paraffin oil overnight, then wring out tightly, wash in lukewarm water and dry. They pick up dust easily and will give furniture a shine.

DUSTING TOOL

Cover upholstered furniture with a large Turkish towel wrung out in water and 1 tablespoon ammonia.

Beat the towel with a broom and the dust will stick to the towel.

DUST MOP, CLEANING
Boil the mop in water with 1 tablespoon of baking soda and 2 tablespoons of paraffin added. Add 10 drops of furniture polish to the rinse water.

Or soak for a few minutes in boiling water and 1 heaped tablespoon of concentrated lye. Rinse several times.

DUSTPAN & SCRAPER
Cut off a third of one side of an aluminum pie plate to make a dustpan and scraper.

DUSTPAN SUBSTITUTE
A sheet of newspaper makes a good substitute if you first wet the edge so it will lay flat on the floor so the sweepings won't slide under it.

FILE TEETH, CLEANING
Apply a thin film of powdered graphite to the file to make it easier to clean.

FLASHLIGHT MAINTENANCE
Insert a wad of aluminum foil between the spring

and the end cap of the flashlight to avoid corrosion and prevent electrolytic action.

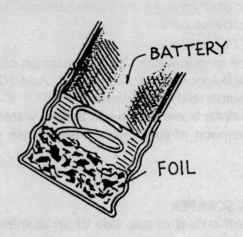

FUNNELS
Strong funnels can be made from clean plastic detergent or bleach bottles. Cut about 4 inches from the bottom, remove the cap, and turn the bottle upside down.

GLASS CUTTING TOOL
Stick a length of friction tape to the underside of the ruler when you use it as a straight-edge for cutting glass. It will not slip around.

GLUE, HOUSEHOLD

Mix a little water with 1 cup of granulated laundry starch until it's of whipping cream consistency. Bring to the boil and allow to cool.

GLUE METAL TO WOOD

Soak the metal in acetone and when dry use household cement to attach it to the wood. Make sure you don't touch the cleaned area of the metal before cementing.

KNIFE BLADE, LOOSE

Remove the blade and clean the tang with a fine emery cloth. Apply epoxy glue and reset the blade into the handle.

MEASURING

Forgot your tape or rule? Any dollar bill measures almost 6 inches long and 2.5 inches wide. Fold it in half for 3 inches and 1.5 inches.

NAILING OR SCREWING INTO HARD WOOD

Rub the nail points with soap, grease or oil before using to lubricate them and hammer lightly.

Another useful lubricator is paraffin wax.

All these methods are also good rust preventers.

NAILING INTO INSIDE WALLS

Warm the nail in hot water for a few minutes, or dip it in melted paraffin, to avoid cracking or crumbling the plaster.

NAIL STARTER

Use a bobby pin to hold the nail so you don't hammer your fingers. A slight pull releases the pin after the nail has started.

Or, if the nail needs to be started too high to reach with two hands, press the nail through a small square of aluminum foil and wrap the foil tightly around the hammer head.

Or cut a strip of lightweight cardboard about 1 inch by 4 inches. Cut a slot in one end with a razor blade. Then you can slip the nail into the slot and use the cardboard as a "handle" as you hammer.

NAILS AND SCREWS, EASE OF HANDLING

Keep a small magnet handy to make it easier to pick up small nails and screws.

NUTS & BOLTS

Rub the threads of the bolt with paraffin wax before putting the nut on the bolt. Then tighten. This will prevent rust and make for easier removal.

PAINT STIRRER

An old dinner fork works great.

POLISHING CLOTH

Use old clean powder puffs for silverware or shoe polishing.

POWER OUTAGE

Paint a dab of luminous paint, or stick luminous tape on flashlights and all tools and equipment you'll need to be able to find easily in a power failure.

PUTTY, HOMEMADE
Mix linseed oil with sifted whiting until it's the right consistency.

ROPE SOFTENER
Old, stiff rope can be made manageable by soaking it in hot soapy water for a while. Once it's soft and pliable, hang it up to dry.

RUBBER GLOVES
If they make your hands sweat, wear a pair of old fiber gloves underneath.

RUBBER GLOVES, LEAKING
Turn the glove inside-out and patch the wear areas (index finger and thumb) with adhesive tape when the glove is new. Glove will last much longer.

SCOURING POWDER SAVER
Cover all but 2 of the holes in the top.

SCREWDRIVER, NON-SLIP
Tape the screw and the screwdriver together with

a small piece of masking tape, and remove the tape after the screw has a good start into the wood.

Or rub chalk onto the screwdriver blade.

SCREWDRIVER, SMALL

Try using the "key" from a sardine can or other small vacuum-sealed can. File the key off just above the slot and file the end to a flat point to fit the screw. Is especially good for small recessed screws.

SCREW STARTER

An old ice pick makes a great starter for small screws, especially in hardwood or plaster. Use the pick to push a starter hold. On very hard wood, tap the pick with a hammer a few times.

SMALL PARTS STORAGE

Use plastic ice cube trays for storing small items. Plastic egg cartons are also useful.

STAPLE REMOVER

Fingernail clippers work great.

STEEL WOOL

To avoid getting splinters, grip the wool in a large

paper clamp and hold the clamp while using.

STEP LADDER SAFETY
Surface the steps with closely-spaced drops of plastic rubber (about 1 inch apart). Make sure steps are clean and dry before applying.

TOASTER, CARE OF
The heating element cleans itself when heated, so needs only the use of a small, clean paint brush to dust away stubborn crumbs. Wipe outside with a damp cloth or mild abrasive.

TOOL HANGER
A good tool hanger when working on a ladder is a C clamp. Clamp it to a side rail.

"C" CLAMP

WAX APPLICATORS, CARE OF

Most wax applicators are made of lamb's wool and should be washed in soapy lukewarm water. Rinse thoroughly and squeeze out excess water, then shake several times while it's drying.

FLOORS, CARPETS, CEILINGS & WALLS

CARPETS, BURNS IN
Use a knife to scrape out the discolored fabric. Then snip some pile from a hidden area of the same carpet, spread it on the palm of one hand and dab glue over it. Press the gluey pile into the damaged spot. When dry the repair should be almost unnoticeable.

CARPETS, CLEANING
Work cornmeal into the pile with a stiff brush, then vacuum well.

CARPETS, MOTHS IN
Add 2 tablespoons of gum turpentine to 1 half-pail of warm water. Dampen a broom with this mixture and sweep the carpets with it.

CARPETS, PINS DROPPED ON
Pins are difficult to find in carpeted areas. Shine a flashlight beam over the floor so the pins will reflect and be easier to find.

CARPET PROTECTION

After spraying rugs and carpet with pesticides, do not walk on them or put any kind of pressure on them until the spray has dried, to prevent them getting a mashed-down appearance.

CARPET STAINS

Clear soda water does a great job at removing wine, coffee and other stains from the carpet. Use as soon as the spill occurs, and rub with a clean cloth or sponge.

Or foaming shaving cream works well for small spills and stains. Just squirt them with the foam.

Or make a paste of starch and buttermilk, spread it over the stain and let it dry before rubbing off.

CARPET STAINS, GREASE

Mix a paste of dry-cleaning fluid and powdered starch. Spread over the stain and let it dry completely. Scrape up the dry dust afterwards, and vacuum. Repeat if necessary.

Or rub dry baking soda into the nap, let it stand, and then vacuum off.

CARPET STAINS, NAIL POLISH

Use amyl acetate (banana oil) to clean up the spill.

CARPET STAINS, OLD

For older stains, mix 2 tablespoons detergent and 3 tablespoons vinegar with 1 quart warm water. Work solution into the stain and blot as dry as possible.

CARPET STAIN PREVENTION

After shampooing, put regular drinks coaster under the furniture legs until the carpet is completely dry, so wooden furniture won't stain the carpet.

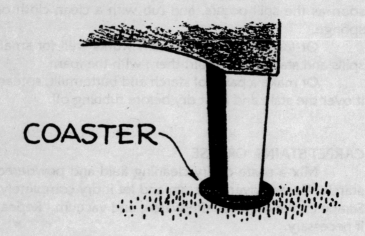

COASTER

CEILING, CLEANING

Use the brush attachment of your vacuum cleaner to clean acoustical tile. Stubborn smudges can be removed with wallpaper cleaner or a cloth slightly moistened with soapy water.

CEILING, STAINED

If you have a water stain on the ceiling, cover it with block magnesia, rubbing the block over the stains until they are covered, and then smooth over with the fingertips.

CEILING TILE, ACOUSTICAL

If the tiles on the ceiling are loose or bulging, if they are applied to wood furring strips, nail them back to the strips with flatheaded nails. If they are applied on plaster, use cement-coated nails, countersinking the nailheads, and cover them with spackle.

FLEA EXTERMINATION

To rid the house of fleas, wet some pieces of wrapping paper with oil of cedar, and scatter them around the floor, under the beds and on the rugs during the night.

FLOOR, PROTECTION

Pesticides used to fumigate your house can damage some floors. Asphalt tiles may dissolve, linoleums may soften or discolor. Parquet flooring can receive a light spraying, but be careful not to dissolve the underlying black cement, which might stain the floor.

FLOORS, WOOD

For stains caused by standing water, rub the area with No. 00 steel wool and then re-wax. If the stain is still there, sand the area lightly with fine sandpaper, and clean the area with No. 1 steel wool and mineral spirits. Let the floor dry, apply a matching finish and feather it out into the surround area. Wax thoroughly when floor is dry. Dark streaks where furniture has stood can be removed with a soapy cloth dipped in paraffin.

FLOORS, WOOD, CLEANING

Clean wood floors with cold tea to give them a beautiful luster.

To preserve the varnish, sprinkle coarse salt over the floor and leave it for 5 minutes before sweeping it off.

LINOLEUM, PAINT STAINED

If the paint is too hard to remove with turpentine or mineral spirits, "sand" it off with very fine steel wool. Be careful to do this gently so the linoleum isn't scratched. Afterwards, wax and polish the area.

LINOLEUM REPAIR

Small holes in linoleum can be filled with a thick paste of finely-chopped cork and shellac. Once it has hardened, sandpaper it smooth and touch it up with matching paint.

MILDEW

Mildew shows on floors as little white spots. Wash the area with soap and water, kerosene and water or 1 teaspoon neutral detergent to a half-pint of lukewarm water. Let it dry thoroughly, preferably in sunlight.

MOTH DAMAGE PREVENTION

If your upholstery has not been treated by the manufacturer with a moth-resistant compound, apply a good protective treatment, available at your hardware store, or hire a professional pest-control company.

ROACH EXTERMINATION

Roaches hate chrysanthemums, which contain a poison deadly to them. Save the blooms and dry them, shred them and scatter them in storage places, behind stationary appliances and other favorite haunts.

Or paint a frequented area with a mixture of lime, water and a little salt.

RUGS, CLEANING

Throw rugs can be washed in the bathtub, using a broom as a scrubber.

Or put them in the tub in soapy water and use the sink plunger to pump the dirt out of them.

RUGS, SLIDING

To prevent a rug from sliding, paint a couple of coats of shellac on the underside.

Or place an old rubber bathmat underneath it.

If you rinse the rug in water containing a little starch, it will be less likely to curl on the floor.

Or wind 3 preserving jar rubber rings together with thread and sew them to the corners of the rug, to form suction cups to prevent sliding.

RUGS, VACUUMING

To vacuum a small rug, use a diagonal stroke. This make it less likely to wrinkle or get caught in the sweeper.

SILVERFISH EXTERMINATION

Buy pyrethrum, an insecticide, and apply it with a powder puff or absorbent cotton onto the baseboards where wallpaper is used. Silverfish feed on wallpaper glue, which contains starch.

TILE, CRACKED

If a vinyl tile becomes cracked, replace it by denting the damaged tile with a hammer to make the edges or the crack curl up. Lift it out of position with a putty knife, scrape the old adhesive from the floor and apply new cement for the new tile. Wait till the cement is tacky to the touch before laying the new tile.

TILE SEALER

When laying vinyl tile, use a heavy roller to make sure the tiles stay flat and permanent. The roller gets rid of air pockets and cements the whole tile.

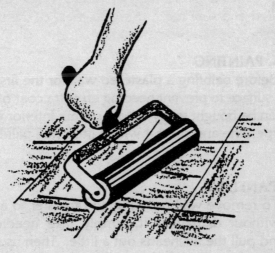

WALLS, CLEANING

To clean kitchen and bathroom walls, try steam cleaning them. In the kitchen, put a large kettle of water on the stove and keep it boiling; in the bathroom run the hot water. Close the door till the room is steamy. This makes the walls easier to clean.

For other walls, mix 1 half cup of ammonia, 1 quarter cup of white vinegar, 1 quarter cup of washing soda in 1 gallon of warm water.

WALLS, MEASURING

To prevent the level from slipping when marking a horizontal line on the wall, fold a piece of sandpaper with the grit side out, and place it between the level and the wall.

WALLS, PAINTING

Before painting a plastered wall for the first time, size the surface to prevent needing an extra coat of paint. Sizing can be bought ready-made, or mix interior varnish with turpentine and color it with a little wall paint.

WALL PANELING

To remove wall paneling and transfer to another room without damaging it, simply take needle-nose pliers and pull the nailheads out a little. Then use a pair of nippers and cut the nailheads off. You can then pry the paneling off the wall. Some repairs to the finish may be needed.

WALL, PAPERING WITH FABRIC

To get the wrinkles out, spray the fabric with water.

WALLPAPER, CLEANING

If you get a spot on the wallpaper, dampen it slightly and cover it thickly with French chalk (obtainable at the drug store), powdered pipe clay or fuller's earth (from the art supply store). Brush it off when dry.

Or rub over the wallpaper with art gum, a loaf of stale rye or other bread, wheat bran sewed in a bag or pipe clay. Overlap your strokes and take care not to streak.

WALLPAPER, METALLIC

To prevent metallic wallpaper from tarnishing, do not use ordinary cellulose paste, which contains chloride, when hanging it. Ask for a non-tarnishing, chloride-free paste.

WALL, PATCHING PLASTER

To roughen the plaster when patching it, use a scraper made from bottle caps nailed to a piece of wood.

FURNISHINGS, DECORATIONS & ORNAMENTS

ANDIRONS, CLEANING

Your fireplace tools can get very dirty and sooty.

Remove deposits with white gasoline (do this outdoors), and wash them with non-gritty kitchen cleanser. Clean out pitted areas with a vinegar and salt solution, rinse and dry. Polish with metal polish.

ASHTRAYS, CLEANING

Instead of washing ashtrays every day, try waxing them. Ashes will not cling, odors will be dispelled, and ordinary tissues can be used to wipe them clean.

Copper or brass ashtrays can be cleaned with denatured alcohol and a stiff brush.

ASHTRAY GLAMOUR

Those inexpensive glass ashtrays, when decorated, can become conversation pieces. Paint the undersides with different enamels of various colors to match the rooms. Use any type of design, modern or traditional, and then varnish them.

If the enamels "creep" on the glass, rub the brush on a cake of soap, then paint.

BEDS, SQUEAKING

If you are annoyed by a squeaking wooden bedstead, pour a small quantity of melted paraffin wax into all the joints and corners. When the paraffin wax solidifies, it will act as an effective lubricant.

BOOKENDS

Temporary bookends can be made from coat hanger wires, very good for small books and magazines. First, straighten the wire, taking out all bends and kinks. Bend into a square, and then fold it over to make an "L" shape.

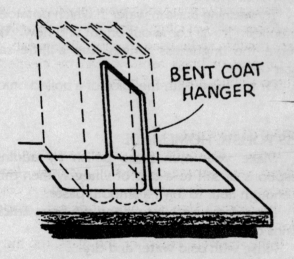

BENT COAT HANGER

Shelf brackets also make fine book ends, and they will look good when painted in gold, silver or other bright colors. Mount the bracket's short end on a hardwood block and paint.

BOOKENDS, SLIDING

If one of a pair of bookends is always sliding, you can usually immobilize it by gluing some wide rubber bands onto the bottom.

BRASS, CLEANING

Try washing brass in water in which potatoes have been boiled. It will come out bright and new. Then, to preserve the brightness longer, rub a little salt and vinegar over it.

Or rub brass with the juice of a boiled onion.

BRASS POLISH, HOMEMADE

Make your own brass polish by adding two tablespoons of salt to a cup of vinegar, then mixing it with enough flour to form a smooth paste.

Dip a damp cloth into it and rub brass article until all stains disappear.

Rinse with cold water and dry.

BRASS, PREVENTION OF TARNISH

To prevent tarnish, give it a protective coat of clear lacquer applied either by spraying it or with a brush. If using a brush, do it carefully to avoid getting the lacquer on nearby finished surfaces, since it may soften up or blister the finish. If using a spray, protect the surrounding area with masking tape and sheets of newspaper.

BRONZE, BROKEN

Broken bronze can be repaired by welding, but if you want to try the job yourself, apply some epoxy glue to the broken edges and press firmly together.

CANDLES, DROOPING

Tall decorative candles often droop and lose their shape during hot weather.

You can prevent this by dipping the entire candle into thinned shellac and then hanging it by its wick to dry.

The shellac will stiffen the candle and prevent its drooping, but will not affect its burning property.

CANDLES, PERFUMED

By lightly coating your candles with cologne, when they are burned later they will add a pleasant fragrance to the room.

COPPER, CLEANING

Clean copper utensils and ornaments with a paste made of a cup of flour and a tablespoon of salt mixed with vinegar. Rub this over the metal and then polish with a bit of flannel or a chamois.

Paint copper with clear shellac afterwards to prevent further tarnishing.

CUSHION FILLER

An excellent cushion stuffer can be made by cutting large plastic bags into strips.

They will hold their shape and spring right back when compressed.

DRAWER BLOCK PULLS

Alphabet blocks can be used for drawer pulls on children's dressers. Use the letter "S" for the sock drawer, "U" for underwear, etc. Use a long wood screw to fasten the blocks from the inside of the drawers.

DRAWER PULLS, LOOSE

If a screw-type drawer pull or doorknob becomes loose, don't use a larger screw to tighten it. This could split either the furniture or the knob, or both.

Instead, remove the screw and fill the enlarged hole with plastic wood or a similar product. When this has set, and before it has hardened, replace the screw.

DRAWERS, SLIDING

To make those hard-to-budge drawers slide much easier, put some thumbtacks on their runners.

DUSTING

Dusting will be finished in a short time if both hands are equipped with dust cloths or mitts at the same time. Makes short work of dusting.

To dust upholstery, cover it with a large Turkish towel wrung out in water with 1 tablespoon of ammonia added. Beat the towel with a broom and the dust will stick to the towel.

FIREPLACE, BRICK

Brick fireplaces can be kept clean and goodlooking longer if you brush the surface of the bricks with liquid wax. Dust won't accumulate as quickly, and it can be whisked off when it does.

To cut down on soot, occasionally throw salt on the logs.

FURNITURE, CEDAR

If your cedar chest or closet loses some of that fresh cedar odor, a fast way of restoring it is by a light sandpapering over the wood. This has a way of opening up the pores of the wood and allows them to "breathe" again.

76

FURNITURE, CLEANING OF OLD

Old furniture that has become dirty or discolored may be greatly improved in appearance by cleaning with a solution of thoroughly mixed vinegar, sweet oil, and turpentine in equal parts. This solution is applied by rubbing vigorously on the wood with a soft cloth. The polish should be shaken before use to assure an even mixture.

FURNITURE, LIMED OAK

You can create a smart and attractive limed-oak furniture finish by stirring one pound of unslaked lime into two quarts of water. Rub this across the grain of the wood and wipe when partly dry (to prevent the accumulation of excess lime). Seal with two coats of thin white shellac, and finish off with a thin coat of paraffin wax.

FURNITURE, MUSTY

Stick some cloves in a green apple and place in drawers.

FURNITURE POLISH, HOMEMADE

An old recipe for furniture polish consists of raw linseed oil and turpentine in equal parts. Or mix equal parts of boiled linseed oil, turpentine and vinegar. The chief thing to remember when using any polish is to apply a very thin coating and then lots of elbow grease. Otherwise, you will acquire a gummy, dust-catching surface.

FURNITURE PROTECTION

Do not write with a ballpoint pen on thin paper on a highly polished table or other fine furniture. You must use pressure on a ballpoint to write, and this will mar and score the fine finish on the furniture. Always put a pad of some kind under the paper when you write.

FURNITURE SCRATCHES

Scratches on dark-colored furniture can often be "obliterated" merely by applying a little iodine to them with a swab of cotton. When this has dried, go over the area with some furniture polish.

Or mix up equal parts of salad oil and vinegar. Keep in a bottle, shaking well before use, and rub this into the wood until the scratches are gone.

If the wood is ebony, use black liquid shoe polish or black eyebrow pencil, following this with furniture polish.

FURNITURE, BROKEN SCREWS IN

When a wood screw breaks off below the surface of the wood, it's usually almost impossible to remove without damaging the wood. Better in this case to drive the screw deeper with a nail set, then fill in the hole with plastic wood, and start with a new screw.

FURNITURE SPOT REMOVER

Those white heat marks made by hot plates on varnished tables are easily removed by rubbing gently with a soft cloth dampened and dipped in cigarette ashes. When they are gone, polish as usual.

If the white stains are caused by alcohol, perfume, etc., they can usually be removed by wrapping a clean cloth around your finger, wetting the tip of it with turpentine, dipping it into cigarette ashes and rubbing it over the spot with a circular motion.

Follow this with a good polishing.

Sometimes, stains will often yield to toothpaste. Put a dab of it on the marks, let stand a few minutes, then rub with a soft cloth. Sometimes a second application may be necessary.

Perfume stains can be removed by applying some cold cream immediately and then wiping it clean with facial tissues.

Crayon marks on smooth surfaces can be removed by rubbing with cigarette ash or metal polish.

FURNITURE, VARNISHED

Varnished woodwork or floors can be given a beautiful luster if they are cleaned with cold tea.

FURNITURE, VARNISHED, CARE OF

The varnish on some furniture is so hard and smooth that the fingermarks and soiled places must be removed with a cloth wrung out of lukewarm suds made with white soap, and the finish restored with a cloth on which a few drops of light lubricating oil have been sprinkled.

FURNITURE, WALNUT

Unvarnished black walnut can be cleaned effectively with a soft flannel cloth soaked in sweet or sour milk.

FURNITURE WASH

To prepare a soapless furniture wash, add three tablespoons of raw or boiled linseed oil and two tablespoons of turpentine to one quart of hot water.

After mixing well, allow to cool and then apply to your furniture with a soft cloth, well wrung out, and covering a small area at a time. Wipe each part dry as you proceed.

Polish the furniture afterwards.

GLASSWARE, ORNAMENTAL OR CUT

Cut glass can be cleaned and brightened with a soft brush dipped in a baking soda solution. Rinse, then dry.

IVORY, STAINED

Remove stains from ivory by rubbing with a cloth dipped in alcohol, and polish with a dry cloth.

Or sprinkle some salt on the stain and then rub with the cut half of a lemon.

Or rub with methylated spirits on a soft cloth.

KNOBS, LOOSE

To tighten loose drawer or cabinet knobs permanently, remove the screw and bend it slightly and replace it. The bend will prevent the knob from turning in the future.

LAMPS, BROKEN BULB REMOVAL

A safe way to remove the jagged end of a broken light bulb from the socket is to take a bottle cork, push it firmly into the broken glass and turn.

LAMPS, FURNITURE PROTECTION

Lamps and ornaments can be padded with the cork inserts from bottle caps to prevent their marring the furniture surface. Use plastic cement to glue the cork to glazed surfaces.

LAMPSHADES, PARCHMENT

Parchment lampshades can be cleaned with a

cloth dampened with soapy water. Another method is to wipe them with a cloth dipped in milk.

To keep them clean, wax them. This will also add a soft luster to them and make them easier to dust.

LAMPSHADE SAVER

Do not use new lampshades without first removing the cellophane covering. The heat from the electric bulbs will contract the cellophane and pull the lampshade out of shape.

LEATHER CARE

Leather furniture should be cleaned annually with mild soap and water. After it is dry, wipe with a good grade furniture cream worked well into the leather, and wipe clean with a dry cloth so there will be no residue to stain clothing.

To remove wax build up, wipe with equal parts of vinegar and water. Indentations caused by pressure from lamps, etc., can be raised by applying lemon oil twice a day for one week, and maintained by applying lemon oil monthly.

MARBLE CARE

Marble tops on tables, lamp bases, and such, may be cleaned by washing with water and synthetic detergent, rinsing carefully, wiping dry, and buffing. If desired, wax them using a pure, white water-wax emulsion, not ordinary floor or furniture wax (automobile paste wax is good) - this helps to retard soil. To polish marble use putty powder or jeweler's rouge.

MARBLE MENDING

To mend broken marble, make a thick paste of Portland cement with water. After cleaning the broken area's edge, apply the cement, press the pieces together tightly, and tie firmly in place until the cement has set.

ORNAMENTS, BOTTLES AS

If you want to remove the neck of a bottle to make the bottle into a lamp or vase, saturate some twine in paraffin, wrap it around where the break should be, then set fire to the cord. When it has burned, pour cold water on the spot. The bottle will come apart cleanly without breaking the whole thing.

ORNAMENTAL MOLDINGS, CHIPPED

If any ornamental moldings on picture frames, furniture or other woodwork become chipped, one easy way to repair them is by rebuilding the missing sections with wood putty. This is sold in powder form, and when it is mixed with water it dries into a hard, wood-like material which can be carved, sanded or sawed.

PAINTINGS, CLEANING

To clean oil paintings, wash a small area at a time with lukewarm mild suds, and dry the area immediately. After the entire surface has been cleaned, go over it lightly with a flannel moistened with linseed oil.

Or rub the surface with the juicy side of a cut onion and allow it to dry outdoors.

If your painting is valuable, use a professional cleaning service.

PHOTOGRAPHS, CLEANING

Photographs can often be cleaned nicely just by rubbing them with a piece of soft bread.

PIANO, CLEANING

Milk is a splendid cleaner for piano keys. Apply on a soft cloth and polish with a clean cloth. See also Ivory, Stained.

Or apply toothpaste to a well-dampened cloth, rub the keys with it, wipe dry and buff with a soft dry cloth.

PICTURE FRAMES

Gilt picture frames can be restored to their former freshness by rubbing them with a small sponge moistened with oil of turpentine, which soon evaporates.

PICTURE FRAMES, ANTIQUING

To get an antique finish on a new picture frame, rub chalk evenly on the new wood. Brush off lightly and apply brown shoe polish all over the frame.

Rub well and the grain of the wood will show up nicely.

PICTURE FRAMING

Pictures can be spoiled by inappropriate framing. The frame should usually be as dark as the middle tone of the picture, and should form a blending between the wall and the picture, so that you are unconscious of the frame when you look at the picture.

For a better job of framing pictures, stick some masking tape or surgical adhesive along the joint between the backing of the picture and the frame, and this will prevent dust and dirt from seeping in.

To give oil-painting effects to prints or magazine covers, paste the picture wet on burlap, then apply a coat of shellac. Frame them in natural color wood without glass.

PICTURE HANGING

It's not a good idea to hang pictures in a room whose walls are covered with the scenic kind of wallpaper, as pictures only add a cluttered, overdone effect.

PICTURE HANGING, PROTECTION OF WALLS

To keep the corners of your picture frames from scratching or marring painted or papered walls, try inserting a thumbtack into the back of the two lower corners. The smooth heads of these tacks will slide easily, leaving no marks on the wall when the picture is shifted for dusting.

POLISHER

Ordinary household cornstarch makes a fine polishing agent for nickel-plate and chrome. Just dampen a cloth and rub it on. When dry, polish with a soft, dry cloth or a chamois.

Old dress patterns are great for polishing mirrors and other glassware. The slight wax content does a great job.

SCREWS, LOOSE

When the wood around screws has worn away and the screws will not hold, wrap the screw with adhesive tape, using as many layers as needed. Screws will hold for a long time.

SILVER, CLEANING

De-tarnish your silver in an aluminum pan containing hot water with a teaspoon each of salt and baking soda for each quart of water. Bring the water to the boil, then put in the silver, keeping the water boiling. After the tarnish comes off (a matter of seconds), wash the silver in soapy water. Polish with a soft, dry cloth. Clean the aluminum pan by boiling it in a weak vinegar solution.

STONE FIREPLACE
To clean a stone fireplace, you'll need a lot of elbow grease and a stiff brush.

TABLE, PAPER STUCK ON
When paper has become tightly stuck on a polished table, pour furniture oil on the paper, let it soak in for a while, and then rub with a soft cloth. The paper should roll off with no damage to the finish at all.

TABLE MATS
Heat-proof table mats can be made by mounting colorful lengths of linoleum on pieces of plywood, cementing the linoleum to the wood and then painting the edges of the wood a cheerful color.

TELEPHONE CLEANING
An ordinary cotton-tipped swab will clean dust and grime from the keypad of your telephone.
Grease marks can be removed with methylated spirit on a soft cloth.

UPHOLSTERY, CLEANING

Vacuum thoroughly to remove loose dirt, especially in crevices. Then whip up thick, dry suds of a mild, synthetic detergent and a little water with an egg beater. Brush the dry suds onto the upholstery, a small area at a time, using only the suds, no water. Wipe the soiled suds off immediately with a damp cloth.

UPHOLSTERY, MILDEW ON

To get rid of mildew on upholstery fabrics, try sponging with a cloth dampened with equal parts of denatured alcohol and water. Allow to dry in the fresh air if possible. This will also get rid of the musty odor in most cases.

UPHOLSTERY, REPAIR

Cigarette burns: darn the hole in close stitches with color-matching yarn, place a damp cloth over the spot and iron the area.

Rips: apply adhesive tape a little longer than the tear, underneath the fabric, sticky side up, and press the torn edges closely together with the raveled threads underneath.

VASE CLEANER

To clean lime deposits and other discoloration from vases and ceramic pieces, scour with a solution of one quarter cup of ordinary table salt dissolved in a small amount of vinegar.

Or clean narrow-necked vases by dropping into them a few dried beans or crushed eggshells. Add a little detergent and water and shake well.

Or clean narrow-necked vases by rolling a double sheet of newspaper into a compact cylinder. Clip and fray one end of this to provide a brush for scouring the bottom and sides of the vase with a cleaning solution.

VASE, LEAKING

Mend a leaking vase by coating the inside with a thick layer of paraffin and allow it to harden. It was last indefinitely.

WASTEBASKETS, METAL

To prevent metal wastebaskets from rusting, wax them inside and out. This will also prevent dust from clinging and they will be easy to clean with a damp cloth.

WOODWORK, PAINTED

When waxing painted woodwork, remember that the wax will have to be removed completely before the trim can be repainted. For this reason, use the liquid self-polishing kind of wax, which can easily be removed with warm soapy water, and will not require the use of strong solvents.

GARAGE, WORKSHOP & CAR

APPLICATORS

Keep a supply of tongue depressors (available at drug stores) in your workshop. They're handy as disposable applicators for glues, etc., and as paint mixers.

ASPHALT TILE, CLEANING

White stains, caused by alcohol spills, can be removed by rubbing the area with baby oil.

AUTOMOBILE, PAINT TOUCH UP

Worn spots on the car finish can be touched up with shoe polish. Rub in with a soft cloth and then cover with auto wax.

AUTOMOBILE REPAIR PAD

Put an old roller window shade in the trunk. Use it on the ground to prevent your clothes getting dirty when your car breaks down.

BASEMENT OR CELLAR, DAMPNESS IN

To find out whether the dampness is caused by

condensation or seepage, attach a pocket mirror to the wall in the middle of one of the damp areas. Leave it overnight and examine it the next day. If the surface of the mirror is fogged or covered with damp moisture, your problem is condensation. If the face of the mirror is dry, but the wall surface is damp, it's seepage.

BATTERY, CAR

To prevent the battery from getting covered with acid, clean the terminals with baking soda and water, let them dry, and paint them with rubber cement. This will help keep the terminals clean and free of acid.

To prevent corrosion, cover the terminals with petroleum jelly, after cleaning them well with water and baking soda, and drying thoroughly.

CAR, CLEANING

Put baking soda on your damp car sponge, or dissolve 2 tablespoons in each quart of warm water, to remove traffic grime and splatters. Rinse afterwards with clear water.

CAR, CLOTHES HANGER FOR

Take a rubber jar ring, crank the rear window tightly on it, and hook hangers onto the ring. Will not scratch the window.

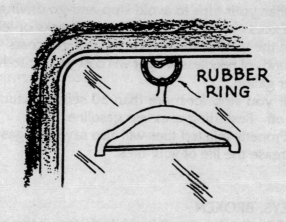

RUBBER
RING

CAR, EMERGENCY LIGHTS

Keep a couple of red toy balloons in your glove compartment with a flashlight. Slipped over the flashlight, the balloon will make an excellent warning light, plus will seal the lens in case of rain.

CAR, FAN BELT SQUEAKING

A drop of glycerin or permanent antifreeze on the fan belt can stop the annoying squeak or noise.

CAR, GAS CONSUMPTION

Jerky driving, fast getaways and excessive speed can burn 50% more gasoline than smooth acceleration. If you drive a stick-shift, the higher gears use less gas.

Plan your trips to avoid stop-and-go driving.

Excess weight, such as luggage racks or leaving things in the trunk, can also add to your gas costs. Each 100 pounds of needless weight will cost you up to half-a-mile per gallon.

If you stop for more than 30 seconds, turn you engine off. Restarting uses less gasoline.

Properly inflated tires will also save you gasoline, and increase the life of your tires.

CAR KEYS, BROKEN

If the key breaks off in the lock, smear the broken end with glue used for mounting sanding disks (obtainable at hardware stores). Push the smeared end gently into the lock so it connects with the broken off piece inside. Withdraw it and the tip of the key should have adhered to the glue and come out with it.

CAR, MAINTENANCE FOR WINTER

Make sure you are topped up with antifreeze at all times.

Keep your battery fully charged for winter, as a fully charged battery needs a much lower temperature before it freezes. Take your battery indoors overnight if weather is really cold.

If you get stuck in the snow without chains, rear tires will give you more traction if you let some air out, but as soon as you're free, get to the service station and refill them.

CHROME, CLEANING

Put peanut butter on a paper towel and rub off the excess.

Or rub with aluminum foil dampened with water, and wipe dry with a soft cloth.

FISHHOOK STORAGE

Imbed extra fishhooks in a block of balsa wood. This will save pricked fingers when reaching into your tackle box, and the balsa wood will float if it drops overboard.

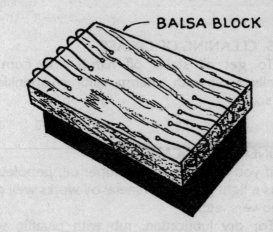

BALSA BLOCK

FLARES

Keep a couple of empty milk cartons in the trunk

of your car. Because of the wax on them, they make good emergency flares if your car breaks down at night. Simply place them at the side of the road, light them and they will burn for 15 minutes.

GASOLINE STAINS ON CAR

A tablespoon of kerosene to 1 cup of water will remove dried gasoline quickly.

GLASS, CUTTING

Stick a length of friction tape on the underside of your ruler when you are using it as a straight-edge when scribing or cutting glass.

HANDS, CLEANING OF GREASE

To get oil stains off hands and from under fingernails, scrub with a damp nailbrush sprinkled with baking soda.

MACHINERY, LUBRICATION OF

If you don't have the proper oil, petroleum jelly works as a light greaser. Mineral oil works well on fans, lawn mowers, etc.

For dry lubrication, rub with paraffin wax, or graphite shavings from a lead pencil.

OILING

To direct oil in hard to get at places, try attaching a stiff wire to the spout of the oil can. Wrap a few turns of the wire around the spout and hold the can so the wire is directly under the spout. Oil will flow along the wire where directed.

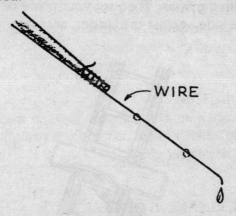

WIRE

OIL STAINS, ON DRIVEWAY

Sprinkle the oil with sand, leave it to absorb the oil for 30 minutes or more, and sweep it away. Or use cleaning fluid.

If stain is old, mix a paste of cleaning fluid and fuller's earth, spread it on the stain and let it dry completely before sweeping it away.

PLASTER, MIXING

Always add the plaster to the water, not the water

to the plaster. It will mix better.

SAWHORSE, TEMPORARY

Use a ladder and a short piece of board. Place the board on the second rung of the ladder so it forms an angle with the floor. Then set your piece of lumber on it with one side against the ladder, and saw.

SAWING

To saw a straight edge with a handsaw, be sure the line you mark is sharp and straight. When starting the cut, guide the saw against the line with your thumb until the groove is formed. Use long, easy strokes and don't bear down on the saw - its own weight should carry it through. Keep your index finger straight along the top edge of the handle. Never twist or bend the saw.

TAR ON CAR
Rub cooking oil or shortening briskly onto the tar, let it stand for a few seconds and rub it off.

TIRES, WHITEWALL, CLEANING
Saturate a cloth with denatured alcohol and a little hydrogen peroxide, apply to the sidewalls. Let it penetrate for a minute or two, repeat the application and rub the dirt off with a clean, alcohol-dampened cloth.

Do not use steel wool or harsh scouring power to remove curb markings, as they can scratch the surface. Instead, apply washing soda with a wet brush, and then rinse.

TOOLS, RUSTY
Remove rust from tools or polished metal by rubbing with a hard typewriter eraser. This will polish out the rust without scratching the surface.

TOOL SHARPENING
If you don't have an oil stone, stroke small hand tools along the striking surface of a box of matches.

TOOL STORAGE
Store small tools in clean, dry sand for the winter to prevent rush and corrosion.

TWIST DRILL SUBSTITUTE

For drilling pilot holes, try using a finishing nail chuck in your electric drill.

WINDSHIELD, CLEANING

Sprinkle dry baking soda on a damp sponge to scour off bugs on your car windshield and wiper blades. Wash windshield inside and out with baking soda and water, then rinse and polish.

WINDSHIELD DEFROSTING

It's a good idea to keep a small jar or box of ordinary kitchen salt in your car during cold weather. Then, if the windshield becomes coated with ice, just rub salt over it to remove.

WINDSHIELD, FOGGING

Rub a cut onion or tobacco from a cigarette butt on the windshield to prevent it fogging.

Use clean blackboard eraser instead of a cloth to wipe steam off. It also fits nicely in the glove compartment.

WINDSHIELD WIPERS

If your wipers aren't working properly, it could be

that there is grease and dirt accumulated on them. Clean
it off with a damp cellulose sponge sprinkled with dry
baking soda.

Or try rubbing the blades with sandpaper to clean
and smooth them.

HOUSEPLANTS & FLOWERS

APHIDS

Pour cool soapsuds over the plant and let a little soapy water trickle into the soil.

ARTIFICIAL FLOWERS

Artificial flowers can be kept in a fixed position in their vases or containers if the stems are placed in sand and hot paraffin wax is poured over the sand.

ARTIFICIAL FLOWERS, CLEANING

Put a few flowers at a time in a large paper bag with a cupful of salt and shake vigorously.

Hold the flowers in the steam of boiling water for a few minutes to freshen them.

CARROTS

Cut about an inch off the large end of a carrot, place it in some water in a shallow container and watch it grow. Makes a lovely fern.

CHRISTMAS CACTUS

Put 2 tablespoons of castor oil around the roots in October. This will help the plant to bloom in December.

CITRUS

Plant a few orange, lemon or grapefruit seeds about half an inch down in the soil in a 4 inch flowerpot. After about a year, they will produce a lovely 7-inch citrus bush.

Lemon leaves can also be used for delicate flavoring in cooking.

CUT FLOWERS, BLOOMING, TO SPEED UP

If you want your flowers to bloom for a certain occasion, place the buds in water and add ice cubes. They should bloom within one hour or so.

CUT FLOWERS, TO DRY

Mix 10 parts white cornmeal with 3 parts borax. Bury the flowers in the mixture. Let them set for 2 weeks. If taken care of, the dried flowers should last for

102

years.

CUT FLOWERS, TO KEEP FRESH

Cut stems with a very sharp knife or scissors, always at an angle. Split the ends of thick stems before putting them in the vase, as it helps absorb moisture. Do not crowd the base.

To keep them fresh, add a teaspoonful of antibacterial compound (the kind used by surgeons when preparing for surgery. It is obtainable at drug stores) to each pint of water in the vase. Because the compound kills germs, you won't need to change the water daily and the flowers will stay fresh longer.

Or try 2 tablespoons of white vinegar and 2 tablespoons of cane sugar in a quart of water.

Or add a little glycerin or a teaspoon of sugar to the water to keep them fresh longer.

Or try aspirins, pennies or ice cubes.

Add a little fresh water every day to keep them fresh longer.

If you refrigerate the flowers every night they'll last longer.

Carnations last longer if the water contains a little boric acid.

Marigolds do well with a little sugar in the water, and will not smell unpleasant.

CUT FLOWERS, WILTING

When they flowers start wilting, cut the end of

each stem with a long slanting cut.

Stand the flowers in hot water for 10 minutes in a dark place, and then quickly move them into deep, cold water.

FEEDING

Put eggshells in a quart of water, let them stand overnight, and water your houseplants with the mixture.

FERNS

To stimulate fern growth, water them once a week with leftover tea.

FLOWER POTS

To make sure the pot won't slide off the window sill, drill a half-inch hole in the sill and inset a short length of wood dowel. Set the flower pot over this peg so it extends up through the drain hole of the pot.

GERANIUMS

Feed geraniums rinsed coffee grounds.

LEAF BRIGHTENING

To brighten green leaf plants, wash the leaves with beer once a week.

PARSLEY

Grow parsley in your kitchen by cutting a porous sponge in half and placing both halves in pretty dishes. Sprinkle a few seeds on the sponges. Keep them moist.

PEACHES

Plant a peach pit one inch down in a pot. It will grow long, thin, willow-like leaves.

PINEAPPLE

Place the top of a fresh pineapple in a pot of water to grow a lovely houseplant.

PLANT MAINTENANCE

To make the leaves of your houseplants shinier, coat the upper sides with milk.

Never oil the leaves of houseplants, as it clogs up the leaf pores so the plant cannot breathe.

Never feed a plant while it's flowering.

Water more frequently in summer than in winter.

PLANTS, TALL

Support tall plants with an inexpensive adjustable brass curtain rod, which can be extended as the plant grows.

POT VALVES

To make sure that soil, roots and water don't leak out of the pot, take an ordinary bottle cap with a crimped edge and place it over the hole before you fill the pot with dirt.

ROSEBUDS

Rosebuds can be persuaded to open by putting a little sugar in the water.

VASES

When shopping for a vase, it's a good idea to choose one in a neutral shade that will blend with any kind of flower. If the vase is to be used purely for decoration, buy one that's colorful, since it will be taking the place of flowers.

VASES, TO MAKE TALLER

To make a vase for long-stemmed flowers, tape two large paper cups together, top to top. Cut the bottom off the top one. Do not fill with water past the taped joint.

WATERING

If you expect to be gone for a few days, put a sponge soaked in water in each flower pot.

Water regularly, but don't let the soil get soggy. Aerate the soil with a fork from time to time.

Stale club soda is good for watering plants.

WATERING CAN

Use a clean plastic bleach or milk jug for small plants. Perforate the cap with a small nail and hammer, and make a small hole in the hollow handle of the jug. Using your thumb over the hole in the handle will help control the water flow.

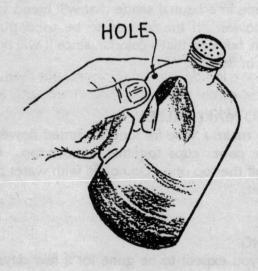

HOLE

KITCHEN

BAKING SODA

Recycle the baking soda in your fridge by pouring the contents down the drains to keep them fresh.

BEATERS, CLEANING

Put egg beaters and potato mashers in cold water immediately and they'll be easier to clean.

Clean the blades with an old toothbrush to get to the difficult spots.

BOTTLES, CLEANING

Cut a lemon into small pieces, put them into the bottle, add a little water and shake thoroughly for a few minutes. Empty the bottle and rinse with lukewarm water.

CABINETS, MAGNETIC PULLS

If the pulls are stiff, try putting a strip of adhesive tape over the magnets. Add more tape if the magnets are still too strong.

If the magnets become weaker later, remove the tape.

CAST-IRON SKILLET, BROKEN

If your cast-iron skillet is cracked or broken, clean the metal thoroughly with steel wool, then coat the edges liberally with plastic steel or epoxy glue, and clamp together. Applying a coat of plastic steel on the outside of the break will add strength. Nevertheless, don't count too much on this mend's ability to withstand extremely hard abuse.

CAST-IRON SKILLET, CLEANING

Clean the outside with a commercial oven cleaner. Let it set for 2 hours and the accumulated black stains can be removed with vinegar and water.

To prevent rust, after cleaning and while the skillet is warm, wipe around the inside with a piece of waxed paper, or rub a small amount of oil on the inside.

CAST-IRON SKILLET, RUSTY

To prevent accumulation of rust, after washing place the skillet back on the stove burner until it gets slightly hot, and then rub it with waxed paper. The wax residue prevents rust.

CATSUP BOTTLE, NEW

To start a new catsup bottle, insert a soda straw into it. This will allow air to get into the bottom of the bottle and make it flow easier.

CHINA, BROKEN

Mix a little pure white lead with linseed oil and use it very thick on the broken edges of the crockery. Press firmly into place, and let the mend set for at least a week before using.

CHINA AND EARTHENWARE, DISCOLORED

To whiten discolored china or earthenware, scour it with baking soda or vinegar and salt.

CHINA, STORAGE

Use the plastic lids from coffee cans as shock absorbers between stacked fine china plates.

CHOPPING BOARD, CLEANING

To remove strong odors such as onion, rub the board with a damp paper towel sprinkled with baking soda.

Or cut a lime or lemon in half and rub the surface with the cut side.

CHOPPING BOARD STABILIZATION

Cut a jar rubber into quarters and glue them on the underside of your cutting board, so it will remain steady when cutting foods.

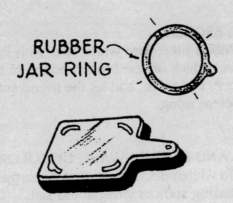

RUBBER JAR RING

CHROME, CLEANING

Dry baking soda and a soft cloth will polish any chrome appliances and fittings. To remove rust spots, rub them with dampened aluminum foil and wipe with a dry cloth.

COFFEE POT, CLEANING

Put in a teaspoon of baking soda, fill the pot almost to the top with water and boil for a while. Rinse the pot thoroughly or scour with equal parts of salt and baking soda.

CONTAINERS FOR FREEZER

Reuse empty coffee cans for freezing vegetables and meats. Line the cans with plastic freezer bags, bringing the bag over the top rim of the cans. Put food in the bag and clamp on the plastic lid, making sure the bag still extends over the edge. Food can be lifted out easily, and can is ready for re-use after scalding.

CORKS

Dip the cork in a little glycerin before replacing it in the bottle. It will help prevent the cork from sticking.

CORK, TIGHT

Soak a cloth in hot water and wrap it around the bottle neck.

CORKSCREW, SUBSTITUTE

A long screw tied to a piece of string works well in an emergency.

DISHPAN, LEAKING

If your plastic dishpan springs a leak, a good temporary repair is to use adhesive tape or bandaid tape over the hole. Make sure the dishpan is clean and dry first. Seal it further by painting around and over the tape with clear fingernail polish.

DISHWASHER

A handful of baking soda in the bottom of your dishwasher (or dishwater) helps to reduce the odor buildup when dishes are left for any amount of time.

DISHWASHING
Sew a large button to one corner of your dishcloth. Use it as a scraper when stubborn food particles stick to dishes.

DRAINS, CLEANING
Pour hot salt water down sinks several times a week to keep them free of grease and odors.

DRAINS, CLOGGED
See *Electrical & Plumbing* section.

DRAINS, MAINTENANCE
Never put coffee grounds down the drain. They clog easily, especially if they get mixed with grease.

EGG STAINS ON PLATES
Rinse egg stains with cold water, as hot water sets them.

FOOD GRINDERS, CLEANING
To clean the food grinder more easily, run a slice

of bread through the chopper after use and before washing. It helps clean the crevices.

FUNNEL

For flour, salt, etc., use a clean envelope. Cut off one bottom corner, and pour into the top opening.

GARBAGE CAN

Heat the bottom of a new or cleaned metal garbage can with a hot iron and drip in a piece of paraffin or candle. The wax will melt and coat the bottom of the container so it will not rust out and can be easily cleaned.

GARBAGE DISPOSAL

Just like the drains in your kitchen sink, an electric disposal should be flushed out periodically with baking soda and hot water to keep it free of grease.

GARLIC PRESS

It's great for mincing ginger and small pieces of onion.

GLASS, CHIPPED

When glassware develops chips on the edges, you can usually rub them smooth again with some fine sandpaper.

GLASS, CLEANING

To clean a bottle or narrow-necked glass vase, drop in the crushed shell of an egg, pour in some hot water, and shake vigorously with a rotary movement for a few seconds. Crushed eggshells also work well cleaning aluminum pans.

Cut glass will shine and sparkle if you use vinegar in the rinse water after washing. Give a final polish with soft tissue paper.

Or clean with a soft brush dipped in baking soda solution. Rinse and dry with a soft cloth.

GLASS, COLD & FROSTED

If you want to serve cold drinks in frosted glasses, fill them with hot water and then pour it out and quickly put them in the freezer for at least 30 minutes. They will then frost up.

GRATER, CLEANING

To clean a cheese grater, rub a crust of hard, dry bread over it before washing.

GREASE, REMOVAL OF

If grease spatters on clothing or wallpaper,

powder the spot immediately with corn starch. This makes it easier to wash or dry clean later.

GRIDDLE

Fill a pump-type plastic spray bottle with cooking oil and use it to mist baking pans, molds, woks and griddles. This will use less oil and it's dripless.

GRIP

Put a few wide rubber bands around slippery bottles or containers to prevent dropping them or spilling.

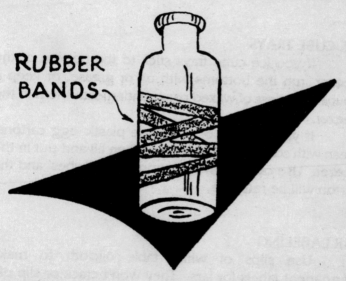

RUBBER BANDS

ICE CUBES, FLAVORED

Try freezing mint in regular-size ice cubes, then using in iced tea. Delicious!

Or freeze fruit juice in cubes or in jello-mold rings. Works well in punch, too. It doesn't dilute the beverage as it melts.

ICE CUBES, LARGE

Convert your muffin tin into an ice cube tray. Large cubes are better when packing ice chests for picnics, and this size also looks pretty in the punch bowl, especially with a sprig of fresh mint or a piece of fruit frozen into each cube.

ICE CUBE TRAYS

If you ice cube trays stick to the bottom of the freezer, rub the bottoms with oil or grease, or keep a double thickness of waxed paper underneath them in the freezer.

If you run out of trays, use plastic egg cartons. Clean with soapy water and rinse, then fill and put in the freezer. Use care when you remove the "cubes" and the carton will be reusable.

JAR LABELING

Use slips of white table oilcloth to make permanent labels for jars. They won't crack or slip off.

Write with ink on the rough side of the oilcloth and then tie the slip around the neck of the jar.

JAR OPENER

A nutcracker makes an excellent "wrench" for opening tight-fitting caps on small-mouthed jars or cans. Apply only moderate pressure, just enough to keep it from slipping. On cans you must be especially careful that you don't squeeze so hard that the top is bent out of shape.

Or try wrapping a cloth round the jar and twisting the ends so you get a better grip. Hold the twisted ends with one hand and unscrew the lid with the other.

KITCHEN, CLEANING

Use a good quality furniture polish on cabinets and kitchen items to protect them from scratches, fingermarks and grease. Dust with a dry cloth to keep them shiny.

Having a party? To make sure your kitchen doesn't become a disaster, place large sheets of aluminum foil in your sink. Empty plates, coffee filter, ash trays, etc., directly onto the foil, fold it up and put it in the trash!

KITCHEN, REDECORATION

To temporarily tint the porcelain of your stove, or of the plastic laminate counter tops, add several drops of desired food coloring and a pinch of detergent to 1 ounce of water, and wipe it on with a clean cloth. The new tint won't come off on dry hands, but will wash away with a wet cloth.

KNIFE, LOOSE BLADE

Remove the blade and clean the tang with fine emery cloth. Apply epoxy glue and reset the blade into the handle.

LIQUIDS, POURING

To pour a fine stream of liquid from a bottle or a can, hold a large nail or pointed lead pencil across the opening before pouring. If done gradually, the liquid will flow down along the sides of the nail or pencil, and will stream evenly off the point into the exact location desired.

MILK STAINS

The lactic acid in milk can easily stain enamel and porcelain. Wipe up spills immediately and clean with cold water.

MIXERS, CLEANING OF BLADES

A toothbrush makes a handy tool for cleaning mixer blades and eggbeaters. It's also good for food graters, choppers, etc.

ODOR, CAULIFLOWER & CABBAGE

Drop a few walnuts, including shells, into the pot when cooking the vegetables to prevent the odor. Or add a little lemon juice or sugar

A piece of stale bread placed underneath the vegetables while cooking will also dispel odor.

ODOR, FISH

To dispel fish odor in your frying pan, sprinkle salt into the pan, add hot water, and let it stand for a few minutes before washing.

Or boil up a mixture of coffee grounds and water.

For silverware, add 1 teaspoon of mustard powder to the dishwashing water. Rub knife blades in a little dry mustard (works for hands, too).

ODOR, IN GARBAGE DISPOSAL

Put a lemon down you disposal unit and switch the unit on.

ODOR, ONION ON HANDS

To remove the odor, rub your hands with raw celery, lemon juice or parsley before washing them.

Or wet hands with clear water and then rub them

with salt.

ODOR, IN PANS
Boil a little neat vinegar in the pan.

OVEN, CLEANING BURNED
Get burned food off the inside of the oven with a cloth soaked in ammonia. Let it stay on the burned areas for a hour or more. The spots should be easy to scrape off afterwards.

OVEN, HEATING
Generally, recipes that take more than 1 hour to cook don't need a pre-heated oven.

If you are using a glass or ceramic baking dish, oven heat can be lowered 20-25 degrees as they retain heat better than other materials.

To heat the oven faster, prevent condensation and rusting inside, leave the door open for about 5 minutes after you light it.

PANS, CLEANING
If the pan is burnt, sprinkle it liberally with baking soda, adding enough water to moisten.

Let it stand for several hours, and the burned portion can usually be lifted straight out.

PANS, DOUBLE-BOILERS

Put a jar lid or some marbles in the bottom part of the double boiler.

When they rattle you'll know the water has boiled away.

PAN LIDS, HOLDING UP OF

When you want to leave the lid on a pan partially open to let the steam out, try a spring-type clothespin and a nail. Drive the nail partly into the side of the clothespin, and clip the clothespin to the edge of the pan. The nail will act as a resting place for the lid.

PANTRY MAINTENANCE

Put plastic lids from coffee cans under syrup, molasses, etc. Makes the pantry much easier to clean.

PASTRY BOARD

Keep an inexpensive powder puff in the flour canister to dust off the pastry board.

PESTLE

A wooden or plastic darning egg makes a good pestle for light crushing. Use any small bowl for the mortar.

PLASTIC CONTAINERS

Clear plastic glasses, etc., can be washed in cream of tartar dissolved in hot water. Soak for a few minutes, rinse and dry.

POTHOLDERS, CLEANING

To keep them clean longer, spray them with starch when new and after each washing. Oil and grease won't stain them as easily.

PLASTIC WARE, SCUFFED

Clean by gently rubbing with a bit of toothpaste on a soft cloth, then wash and dry.

PLASTIC WARE, STAINED

If tea or coffee or similar has stained the insides of plastic cups, scour them with a paste of baking soda and water. If you rinse them out well after use, they won't stain as easily.

Or try cream of tartar dissolved in hot water. Soak them for a few minutes, rinse and dry.

Sorry, stains that have penetrated the plastic are not removable.

PLATES, STORAGE

To stand your plates or platters on edge in kitchen

cabinets, try making small mats of sandpaper for the shelves.

This will prevent the plates from slipping.

POTHOLDERS

Make knitted potholders from leftover yarn, or sew them with leftover fabric.

Attach potholders to your apron with a large snap - keeps it handy!

POTS & PANS, CLEANING

If milk or any other food sticks in pots and pans while cooking, sprinkle scouring powder into the vessel, cover with water, and leave overnight.

Your washing process the next day will be easy.

Or try a solution of equal parts hot water and ammonia.

Scrub with a plastic scouring pad.

With aluminum pans that are stained black with use, try grapefruit and/or lemon peels for a cleanser.

Boil peel in the pan for half an hour and then wash as usual.

RECIPE CARDS, HOLDER FOR

Place a fork upside down in a tumbler and put the card between the tines.

RECIPE FILE

Old or new envelopes can be used as a file. Use the tabs sticking up for labeling, and place in the box the envelopes came in.

REFRIGERATOR, CLEANING

Don't use harsh cleaners to scrub off messy smears and sticky fingermarks on the fridge. A cleaning wax will do an efficient job and also leave a wax coating that will protect the surface and resist dirt.

Or, to clean an old fridge, mix 2 tablespoons of silver polish paste, 1 teaspoon of liquid bleach and one teaspoon of liquid detergent.

REFRIGERATOR, DEODORANT FOR

Dispel odors by pouring a little vanilla on a piece of cotton and keeping it inside a compartment.

REFRIGERATOR, MILDEW IN

To prevent mildew inside, or on the gaskets, wipe over with vinegar. The acid destroys the mildew fungus.

ROLLING PIN

A large olive jar or other cylindrical glass jar works great as a rolling pin and can even be filled with water for extra weight.

SALAD BOWL, WOODEN

Wooden salad bowls can develop a mellow odor with age, and the flavor of the garlic is preserved if the bowl is not washed.

126

Drain the bowl after use, dry with absorbent paper and polish with oiled paper. Store in a cheesecloth bag.

To clean, use a dry method, as the wood with become discolored with water if it hasn't been finished with shellac or varnish.

Scrub the inside of the bowl with fine, dry sand, using a circular motion in the direction of the grain. Follow with a very quick rinse under the cold water faucet and dry thoroughly with a towel.

Cracks can be repaired with shellac.

SCISSORS, TO SHARPEN

Try cutting through sandpaper or steel wool several times.

SCRAPER

An old wooden mixing spoon can make an excellent scraper if you cut off half the bowl and bevel the scraping edge.

Oil it frequently so foodstuff won't stick.

SHAKERS, SALT & PEPPER

If you have a shaker that delivers too quickly and too much, wash the shaker out thoroughly and dry it. Then stop up some of the holes with fingernail polish.

Lost the corks? Try using adhesive tape to close the hole.

SHELVES, LINING

Cut 3 layers of shelf paper and put them down all at one time. As the top one becomes soiled just strip it off and a clean one is already there for use.

Or try using thin plastic sheets (non-stick), obtainable at hardware stores. These can be taken out periodically and washed.

SILVERWARE CLEANER

Save that cooking water from the boiled potatoes. Soak your silverware in it for about an hour and it will come out just like new. Badly tarnished silverware can be cleaned by rubbing with a piece of raw potato smeared with baking soda.

SINK, STAINED

Mix scouring powder containing bleach into a paste with water, rub over sink and leave it overnight. Rinse it away next morning and the sink should be sparkling.

SINK, RUSTY STAINLESS STEEL

First rub the rust with lighter fluid, and then give it a treatment of scouring powder. The sink should be restored to a bright newness.

SPONGES, SYNTHETIC

To make your kitchen sponge last longer and smell fresher, soak it overnight in a solution of 4 tablespoons of baking soda to a quart of water.

STAINLESS STEEL, CLEANING

Wash as usual with detergent, then apply mineral oil with a soft cloth. Wipe off the excess.

STAINLESS STEEL, SCRATCHED

Scratches can be minimized by rubbing over them with baby oil.

STORAGE

Make a lazy susan for your cabinet by taking a tin or aluminum pie plate, putting a nail through the center, with two small washers underneath. Works great!

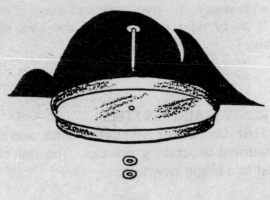

Organize your spices alphabetically - makes it easier and faster to find one when you need it.

A screen door spring or other light tension spring can be used to hold paper bags of all sizes ready for use. Fasten the spring with two small screws to the inside of a cabinet door.

STORAGE, RECIPES

Take 2 thumb tacks and a couple of rubber bands. Tack the bands, stretched, to the back of a cabinet door. They will hold loose recipes and papers in place.

STOVE BURNERS

Have the markings worn off the dials? Use colored nail polish to mark "F" for front and "R" for rear.

TEA KETTLE, CARE OF

To prevent sediment accumulation, when you've finished using the kettle, always empty it of water. Rinse with cold water before using it again.

THERMOS BOTTLES

A method of getting the inside of a thermos bottle thoroughly clean is to fill it with warm water to which a heaping teaspoonful of cooking soda has been added, and letting it stand overnight. Do this at least once a week with bottles that are used regularly.

131

LAUNDRY, STAINS & CLOTHING

BAGGING

If pants or skirts bag, lay the garment on the ironing board and gather fabric to approximately the right size. Lay a damp cloth over top and press with a hot iron to shrink away the excess fabric.

BLANKETS, CLEANING

Add a cup of moth balls or crystals to the rinse water when you wash blankets before storage.

Or add 1 ounce of turpentine to the wash water. Odor evaporates after a while.

To keep blankets feeling soft, add a teaspoon of glycerin to each pint of rinse water.

BLANKETS, STORAGE

To store woolen blankets, put newspapers and a scattering of yellow soap between the folds. This will guard them again moth invasion, as the soap doesn't evaporate like mothballs, and leaves no smell.

BLEACH SUBSTITUTE

Try regular rubbing alcohol in lukewarm water to

take away dirt, ice cream and chocolate stains. It will not take any color out.

For white fabrics, sunshine is still the best.

BLEACHING

White linens: Use 1 cup of bleach to a large pan of water. Soak the material for 1 hour.

BRIGHTENING

Add a few drops of turpentine to lukewarm water and soak delicate colors in it before washing them in sudsy water.

For colored clothes, add a half-cup of household ammonia to the rinse water.

BUTTONS

Dental floss makes a great thread for attaching buttons to men's work clothes and children's play clothes. It's much stronger than regular thread and can handle rough treatment.

Paint buttons, thread and all, with clear nail polish to seal the thread.

CHIFFON, WASHING

Use pure soap, and do not rub the fabric, just rinse up and down in not-too-hot water.

CLOTHES PINS, DIRTY

When wooden clothes pins get black, boil them in a weak solution of bleach and water for a few minutes.

Plastic clothes pins can be washed in warm sudsy water with a little bleach.

COLOR, PRESERVATION OF

Add vinegar to the rinse water to hold colors better.

COTTON, TO WHITEN

Boil the white cotton garment in water to which slices of lemon have been added.

CREASES, REMOVAL

To remove creases, hang item in a steamy bathroom.

Or put the article, dry, in the tumble dryer for a few minutes with a damp sponge.

DEODORIZER FOR CLOTHING

To get rid of odors such as cigarette smoke, hang the clothing on a hanger on the shower curtain rod or near the bathtub. Half fill the tub with hot water and add vinegar. Close the door and let the vinegar steam the odor away.

DRYING "DRIP-DRY"

Place the plastic garment bag from your dry cleaner over a hanger. Hang the clothing over this and clothes will dry much faster and with fewer wrinkles.

First, though, make sure the bag doesn't have printing on the outside. If it does, simply turn the bag inside out before using it.

FADING

If you are airing delicate clothes in the sun, fasten an old towel over both sides so they get less direct sunshine.

Soak cotton fabrics in a strong solution of salt water overnight before you wash them.

FRAYING:

Cloth belt: if you have a belt with frayed holes, go around the edges of the holes on both sides of the belt with clear nail polish. Renew as needed.

Gloves, wool: put glycerin or lemon juice in the final rinse water when cleaning them to prevent it.

FUR, CLEANING

For white furs, rub in cornstarch or 50/50 mixture of flour and salt. Shake it out well, so that the cornstarch doesn't leave a residue on anything you walk near.

GLOVES, CLEANING OF

Cotton: wear them when you hand wash lingerie and pantyhose.

Wool: to prevent fraying, put glycerin or lemon juice in the final rinse water.

GLOVES, REPAIR OF

With kid gloves, mend them with cotton thread, as it won't tear the leather.

HEM MARKS

To get rid of the line from a let-out hem, rub with a vinegar and water solution.

IRON, TO CLEAN

Dip a damp cloth in baking soda and run over the bottom of the iron. If the iron is very sticky, pour salt onto a piece of brown paper and iron it. Then iron a piece of waxed paper.

Or rub with powdered whiting or pumice and fine steel wool.

Or rub with slightly dampened salt and a piece of crumpled paper.

Rub burned-on patches with a heated solution of vinegar and salt.

Wax buildup can be removed with very fine sandpaper. Polish with fine soapless steel wool and wipe off with a damp cloth.

The outside can be cleaned with toothpaste or silver polish.

Corrosion can be removed by filling the iron with vinegar and letting the iron get very hot. Pour out the vinegar and from then on always use distilled water in the iron.

The holes in the bottom can be cleaned with a pipe cleaner dipped in a solution of detergent and water.

IRONING BOARD MAINTENANCE

Put heavy duty aluminum foil under the regular cover. The reflected heat will make the ironing much easier.

IRONING TECHNIQUE

First, iron parts that hang off the board (cuffs, sleeves, belts, etc.). Then, iron the body of garment.

Cuffs: if a shirt has double cuffs, don't crease the cuff with the iron. The cuffs can be folded over when the shirt is put on and they'll wear much better.

Lace: don't bother. Simply roll smoothly around a clean, round bottle after washing and let it dry.

Tablecloths: press only a center crease, as creases do not lie flat on the table. Then fold by hand for storage.

Shine, unwanted: got shiny areas on jackets or pants? Try sponging with vinegar before pressing.

Or use a steam iron covered in an old, cotton

sock, pulled tight.

Sleeves, puffed: Turn the garment inside out, slip a folded towel under the puffs and quickly press with a warm iron.

Starching: Turn off the steam to get a better finish.

IRON-ON PATCHES

To remove, set your iron to HOT or COTTON and rub the entire patch with the iron. While the patch is still hot, pull it off.

JEANS

A blue-ink ballpoint pen (or black for black jeans) will put the color back into small faded spots in blue jeans, or into the white line when you change the hem.

Or try using a blue crayon and press with a hot iron afterwards.

JEWELRY PROTECTION

If you want to wear a heavy pin, take a piece of felt and fasten the pin to your clothing through the felt.

KNITTED CLOTHING, STRETCHED

Put item on the ironing board and spray with water. Pat back into shape and leave overnight to dry.

LACE, PRESERVATION

When old lace becomes yellow, whiten it again by washing it in sour milk. Let dry and then rinse in cold water.

LACE, WASHING

To protect fine lace, put it in a jar of soapsuds. Seal the jar firmly and shake vigorously.

Use a solution of sugar and water to starch fine lace.

LAUNDRY LOGISTICS

If you have to go to the laundry room or laundromat, fill a sock with detergent instead of taking the whole box.

LINT PREVENTION

To prevent them picking up lint in the washer or dryer, before washing, place small dark articles such as socks and scarves in an old nylon stocking and tie a knot at the end.

LINT REMOVAL

Tie a few strips of nylon net together into a small ball. Rub over lint.

For lint in creases of clothing, fold an ordinary pipe

cleaner and apply.

LOST MATES
To keep children's gloves and shoes in matching pairs, clip them together with a clothespin. Print the name of the child on the clothespin or use a dot of colored nail polish as an identification mark.

NAME TAGS
Write the name on the article with an ordinary crayon, and then press, with a medium iron, over the writing on the wrong side of the article. Color will be set and won't wash out.

NYLON FABRICS
Add a few drops of vinegar to the rinse water to prevent the fabric becoming grey or dingy-looking.

NYLONS
Match odd shades of nylon stockings by placing them in a pan of boiling water with 1-2 tablespoons of salt. Boil for 10-15 minutes.

NYLONS, MAINTENANCE
Add a little vinegar to the rinse water to increase

elasticity and help prevent runs.

PANTS, CREASES
To sharpen pants creases, rub along the wrong side with a bar of soap, then press with a damp cloth on the right side, making sure you iron along the original creases.

PERFUMED CLOTHING
Add a few drops of your favorite cologne to the final rinse water.

Or store unwrapped perfumed soaps in your clothing drawers.

PERFUMED LINENS
Store perfumed soaps, unwrapped, among your linens.

PILLOWS, FOAM RUBBER
Remove the covers and dunk them in clear, cold water (no soap). Slowly squeeze out the water. Repeat until the water runs clear.

REPAIRS, RIPS & TEARS
Use iron-on mending tape in a matching color.

Also, press using a damp cloth even if you have a steam iron.

SEWING DRAPES

Allow a double hem on curtains and drapes to allow for shrinkage when washing, and to help them hang straight.

SEWING ELASTIC

To replace elastic, sew the new piece onto the end of the piece being removed. As you pull the old piece out, the new one is automatically pulled into place.

SEWING HEAVY FABRIC

If you're sewing stiff fabric, stick the needle occasionally into a bar of soap. The soap will lubricate it and make the going much easier.

Or rub the seams in advance with a bar of hard soap for the same effect.

SEWING HEMS ON CLOTHING

Use a sink plunger as a guide to marking a hem line. Stand it upright and mark in pencil or chalk on the handle where the hem line should be. It leaves both hands free and will remain in one position.

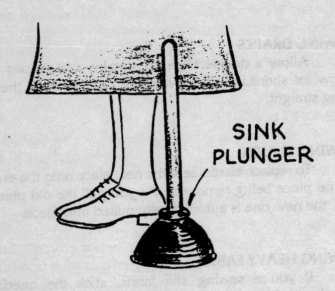

SINK
PLUNGER

SEWING, SEAMS

Use strips of masking tape instead of thread to baste two pieces of cloth together before sewing the seam. Apply across the seams as close together as required to keep the edges together. Remove the strips while sewing, ahead of the needle.

SHOWER CURTAINS, PLASTIC

To prevent them from becoming stiff, wash in

warm sudsy water and rinse in water containing a little glycerin or mineral oil. Add a few drops of vinegar to the rinse water to reduce dust collection. If the curtains are wrinkled when dry, lay them on a smooth surface, cover with magazines and leave overnight. This should make them look as if they are ironed.

SHRINKING & SETTING

To shrink a piece of material and set the color at the same time, mix a pint of salt in 4 gallons of water and soak the fabric for at least an hour.

SILK, MAINTENANCE

When black silk clothing has become worn and shiny, sponge with strong black coffee and then iron on the wrong side. This should improve the appearance.

SOCKS, MAINTAINING

Rub paraffin wax on the heels and toes of socks before they are first worn and after every washing. This makes them last longer.

SOCK SORTING

Pin socks together with a safety pin before washing. That way you won't "lose" one.

STAINS

Acid: for nonwashable fabrics, immediately sponge off with water. Add a few drops of ammonia or white vinegar to restore the color if fabric is colorfast. Or apply baking soda to both sides of the fabric, allow to stand and then sponge off.

Adhesive tape: use cleaning fluid for both washable and nonwashable fabrics.

Alcohol: soak fresh stains in cold water with a few tablespoons of glycerin added. Rinse with white vinegar and water. Always treat immediately, as the stains will go brown over time. Nonwashable fabrics can be sponged with denatured alcohol.

Ammonia: may bleed dyes or cause color changes in fabric. These can be corrected by applying white vinegar and water to the affected areas.

Automobile grease: apply a small piece of butter, then launder.

Banana: cover the spots liberally with a paste of fuller's earth and water. Let it dry thoroughly and then brush off.

Beer: beer is water soluble. Launder as usual. For nonwashables, sponge with a cloth dipped in soapy water. For old stains, add a little ammonia to the wash water.

Blood: cover the spot immediately with a paste of cornstarch and water. Rub it on and place article in the sun to dry. Brush the cornstarch off when dry. Repeat as necessary.

On silk, moisten a few inches of white sewing silk

145

with your tongue, roll thread into a ball and rub gently over the stain.

On nonwashable fabric, soften the stain with a castor oil solution, then sponge with warm water. If stain persists, add a few drops of ammonia to the solution.

On mattresses, cover with a starch paste and remove when paste has dried. Repeat as necessary.

Candy (except chocolate): use plain cleaning fluid (or peroxide on white fabric).

Catsup: on washables, sponge with cool water and let stand for 30 minutes. Work detergent into the stain and rinse as usual.

Cheese: treat with cold water.

Chocolate: for nonwashables, soak for a few minutes in a solution of rubbing alcohol in lukewarm water. Or try carbon tetrachloride and then sponge with warm water. Tough stains can be treated with pepsin powder. Let stand for 30 minutes and sponge with warm water.

For washables, wet the article and rub borax soap powder into the stain. Roll garment up, lay aside for 15 minutes and then scrub with a brush. Or try glycerin on the stain and wash with clear water. Repeat as necessary.

Coffee: Stretch fabric over a bowl and pour boiling water over the stain from a height of 2 feet. If necessary, cover stain with glycerin and repeat.

Dye transfer: maybe caused by unstable dye, excessive agitation in the washing machine, or too hot a water temperature when laundering. If fabric is white, use a fabric color remover, and launder. If dye remains, launder again with chlorine bleach (if safe for fabric) or all-fabric bleach. Launder again.

Fabric softener (blue liquid): may be caused by putting softener directly onto fabric. Rub dampened stain with bar soap and then launder. Or wash with warm or hot water and 4-6 cups of soap powder (not detergent). Rinse twice in cold water. Repeat as necessary.

Fabric softener (dryer sheets): these may be caused by having either too small a dryer load, or too hot a dryer temperature. Rub dampened stain with bar soap and launder. Or wash with warm or hot water and 2 cups of soap powder (not detergent). Rinse twice in cold water. Repeat as necessary.

Fruit: If warm water doesn't remove stain, sponge with cold water and a few drops of glycerin. Let stand for 3 hours, then sponge with vinegar. Rinse in clear water.

On linens and tablecloths, stretch stained area over a bowl or sink and pour boiling water over the fabric from a height of 8-10 inches.

On white woolens, soak the stain for 10-15 minutes in 1 quart of lukewarm sudsy water with a tablespoon of hydrogen peroxide added. Rinse in lukewarm water, then dry.

Glue: On washables, soak item in warm water. On nonwashables, dampen stain, sponge with vinegar, and rinse.

Grass: these can be tough. Ordinary rubbing alcohol works well on cotton and most colorfast material, but test a corner first. Rub alcohol on stain until it disappears and then wash as usual.

Gravy: Sponge with carbon tetrachloride,
followed by lukewarm water. Or use cornstarch.

Grease: rub liquid detergent lightly on the stain.
Rinse or wash as usual. If the stain is deep, work the
detergent through the fabric by holding with both hands
and bending the individual fibers so they rub against each
other. Rinse thoroughly. Also, add a little borax to the
wash water.

Or sprinkle with talcum powder or cornstarch, rub
well into stain, and let it stand until the powder has
absorbed the grease. Brush off and repeat if necessary.

Automobile grease responds well to butter,
followed by regular wash and rinse.

Ice cream: soak for a few minutes in a solution of
rubbing alcohol in lukewarm water.

Ink: if stain is ballpoint ink, place stain face down
on kitchen towels; sponge the back of the stain with dry
cleaning solvent. Rub with bar soap, rinse and launder.

Or apply hair spray liberally to the stain. Rub with
a clean dry cloth and the ink will usually disappear.

Or rub with alcohol before laundering.

If stain is regular ink, dampen it with water and
rub with bar soap. Rinse, then soak in all-fabric bleach in
hottest water safe for fabric. If stain persists, launder
using chlorine bleach, if safe for fabric.

Permanent ink cannot always be removed. Try ink
remover from the hardware store or office supply store,
but you may not be successful in removing the stain.

Iodine: apply sweet milk to the stain.

Discoloration usually disappears when dry. Repeat if necessary.

Lipstick: rub a slice of white bread over the stain. When you brush away the crumbs the lipstick should also go.

Or, for washables, wash in hot water and soap. With non-washables, try cleaning fluid and press with a clean white blotter. Blotter should absorb the lipstick.

Mildew: Soak for a few minutes in sour milk or lemon juice and follow with a hot sun bath. Repeat as necessary. Or rub the stain well with a freshly cut tomato, cover with salt and place in direct sunlight to dry. For white fabrics, moisten with a mixture of lemon juice and salt and spread in the sun to bleach.

Milk: moisten stain with warm water, apply powdered pepsin and work into the fabric with a glass rod. Let stand for half an hour and then sponge with water.

Mud: wait till the mud is dry and try brushing it out. If traces remain, launder as usual, or if article is nonwashable, sponge with clear water.

Mustard: On washables, apply glycerin and then wash with soap and water. On nonwashables, apply warm glycerin and sponge with water. If this fails, use diluted denatured alcohol.

Nail polish: apply amyl acetate (banana oil) immediately.

Oil: Lubricate before washing with dishwashing liquid, or an equal parts mixture of glycerin and warm water. Let stand for 10 minutes before washing.

warm water to flush the paint out, while it is wet. Launder. If the paint dries, it cannot be removed.

Oil-based paint, varnish: apply recommended solvent mentioned on the paint container. Or apply turpentine, then rub with bar soap. Rinse and launder.

Peach: cover the area with salt, let stand for 24 hours and wash in lukewarm water.

Pencil, indelible: soak the stain in 1 part denatured or rubbing alcohol to 2 parts water, and then launder.

Perfume: wet the area with water, then work on it with glycerin and a cheesecloth. Rinse with water. If traces are still there, work on it some more with a 20% solution of vinegar, and flush with water. Or, on linen, put hydrogen peroxide on the stain and then launder.

Perspiration: On woolens, add a little vinegar to the last rinse water. It will also give woolens new softness and sheen.

On other fabrics, especially dark ones, dissolve a cup of salt in hot water and sponge until the stain disappears.

You can also try flushing fresh stains with detergent and water, followed by ammonia in solution. For old stains, use a mixture of water, detergent and vinegar.

On mattresses, sponge with warm water with a few drops of vinegar added.

Rust: squeeze lemon juice onto the spots, pat them with salt and hang the clothing in the sun.

On white washables, cover the stain with cream of

tartar, and gather up the ends of the article so the stain stays as the bottom, so the powder stays on it. Dip all of it into hot water for about 5 minutes. Launder as usual.

Scorches: Light scorches can be removed from linens by first wetting the stained areas with cold water and then exposing them to the sun until the scorch disappears.

On cottons, wet the stain with water and cover with a thick paste of laundry or corn starch. After it has dried, sponge it off with peroxide, iron the article, and put into the sun for a few hours.

On woolens, apply hydrogen peroxide and then place the stained area in the sun. Watch from time to time until stain is gone. If necessary, apply more hydrogen peroxide as it dries out. If the dye begins to lighten, stop the procedure and rinse the peroxide from the fabric.

Shoe polish: Use rubbing alcohol or carbon tetrachloride.

Soil, general: may be caused by greasy stains attracting dirt, filling washing machine too full, not using enough detergent or too cool a water temperature. Use a prewash spray and launder with hottest water safe for fabric.

Tar: rub kerosene or lard on the stain, let it stand for an hour or more and then wash the fabric in the usual way.

If it's nonwashable fabric, sponge with cleaning fluid.

Tomato juice: sponge thoroughly with cold water

to dissolve solid particles, work glycerin into the stain and wash or sponge with soap and water. Finish with a good rinsing.

Urine: Wash in a solution of warm, soapy ammonia and water.

Varnish: saturate fabric with turpentine or mineral spirits, rub stain between hands and then sponge with alcohol.

Water: rub water rings gently with a silver spoon or coin.

Wax, candle or crayon: Scrape off surface wax with a dull knife, and then sponge it out with carbon tetrachloride, or dry-cleaning solvent, by flushing it out onto a towel (or kitchen towel) placed underneath. If necessary, use petroleum jelly or white mineral oil to lubricate the stain, and then sponge with carbon tetrachloride again.

If the clothing is washable, crayon traces can be removed with soap and ammonia, but be careful with colored items. Launder with soap powder (not detergent) and 1 cup of baking soda.

Wine: on table linens, cover stain immediately with salt, then proceed with your meal. Stretch stain on washable fabric over a bowl and secure with a rubber band. Sprinkle salt over area and pour boiling water on it from a height of 2-3 feet.

For nonwashables, try fuller's earth or cornstarch. Let it stand for a while then brush off.

Yellowing: you may be using too much soap when laundering. See also *Yellowing*.

STARCH SUBSTITUTE

Save the water from cooking rice. Keep it in the refrigerator and use just like regular starch.

Or dissolve granulated sugar in water.

SWEATERS, CLEANING

White sweaters can be cleaned without washing by rubbing them in a mixture of 1 part salt to 2 parts cornmeal, Let them stand overnight and then brush thoroughly.

When hand washing sweaters, put a capful of creme hair rinse in the final rinse water.

Speed up drying by rolling the sweater in a Turkish towel and pressing out excess water with a rolling pin.

SWEATERS, UPKEEP

Brush synthetic fiber sweaters with a nylon bristle hairbrush to smooth out matted or fuzzy areas.

Sew elastic thread around the necks of new children's sweaters to prevent them from stretching out of shape.

VELVET, CLEANING

For water spots, remove by sponging with cleaning fluid, always rubbing in one direction.

WASHER OVERFLOW

Too many suds? Sprinkle in some salt and the bubbles will vanish.

WATER, SOFTENING OF

To soften the water for washing woolens, add a little ammonia.

WOOLENS, CLEANING

Rinse with 1-2 tablespoons of glycerin in lukewarm water.

WOOLENS, STORAGE

Store small woolen items in paper bags and seal with adhesive tape. Mark what's in the bag on the outside.

YARN, RE-USING

When unravelling yarn from hand-knitted garments, wind it onto a wire coat hanger with the curved ends pushed in.

Leaving it on the hanger, wash in soapy water and hang it up to dry.

After drying thoroughly, rewind the yarn into balls. It will have no tangles and will be like new.

It will have no tangles and will be like new.

YARN, STORAGE
Put the yarn in a paper bag and mark the outside with a description.

YELLOWING, PREVENTION OF
Wrap seldom-used white linens in blue tissue paper to prevent yellowing.

Or place a few small pieces of camphor gum in the linen closet.

If yellowing has occurred, let the linen soak in buttermilk for 2-3 days.

ZIPPER REPAIR
If the pull handle is lost or broken, use an ordinary paper clip. Just insert the clip through the hole at the top of the sliding portion.

ZIPPER, STICKING
Rub a lead pencil over the stuck teeth. Or, try a wax candle.

ZIPPER PROTECTION
To avoid damaging a nylon zipper with a hot iron, place a double thickness of medium-weight woolen

MISCELLANEOUS

BABY HINT

Use the same perfume in the hospital and when you get home, so your baby starts to identify with it. When you get home, dab a little on the crib sheets or pillow. Your baby will smell the "mother" smell and feel warm and safe, so you can get a little extra sleep.

BALLPOINT PENS

If your ballpoint pen starts to skip, as if it has run out of ink, try heating it by holding the point against a lighted electric light bulb for a minute. This loosens clogged ink.

BEDDING & CLOTHING, WORN OUT

Tear off the selvedges from worn out shirt hems, sheets, etc. They are strong and make great ties for newspaper bundling and plants in the yard, etc.

BOOK MARK

Use an ordinary wire coat hanger as a book mark. Slip it over the book, or magazine, with the handle upwards, and the flat, bottom wire underneath the book, to keep the page open where you want it.

BOOKS, MOLDY

Clean moldy leather book bindings with a cloth dampened in ammonia, or sponge with denatured alcohol and dry in the sunlight.

Or try dusting the paper with cornstarch and allowing it to remain on for several days before brushing it off.

To prevent mold, put a few drops of lavender oil in the bookcase.

BOOKS, SOILED

To clean soiled edges of rarely-used books, press a lump of modeling clay over the spots repeatedly, kneading frequently. Clean one small area at a time and do not rub. Or try lightly sanding the edges. Put the sandpaper on a curved block which has the same curvature as the book edges. For grease stains on cloth covers, rub lightly with carbon tetrachloride.

BOOKS, TORN PAGE

Torn book pages can be mended by painting the tear with egg white. Leave the book open until it is absolutely dry.

BOOKS, WARPED

Set warped books on a flat surface in the humid atmosphere of your bathroom, place a board on top and leave them weighted down for a few days.

CANDLES

Candles will burn slower, hold shape better and give a brighter light if placed in the refrigerator for a few days before use.

CHALK & CRAYONS, CARE OF

Wrap the upper part in masking tape to save getting things dirty and dusty.

DARNING

Use a flashlight instead of a darning egg when

darning socks. The light will make the job easier on your eyes.

DECAL REMOVAL
It's easier to remove decals if you first paint them with several coats of hot vinegar. Allow the vinegar plenty of time to soak well into the decal and then simply wash the decal from the surface.

ENVELOPE SEALER
Tired of licking envelope flaps? Wrap an ice cube in a lightweight, clean cloth and use it to moisten the flaps. It should melt just fast enough to keep the cloth dampened enough.

EXERCISING
Use your ironing board as a slant board by placing the small end on a sturdy box about 18 inches high. Great for sit-ups!

FACIAL CLEANSING
After cleansing, spray your face with cold mineral water.

After having applied makeup, spray your face with mineral water, or put mineral water on a tissue and lightly dab it all over your face. This helps makeup stay fresh longer.

FACIAL MASK, HOMEMADE

Grind 1 tablespoon wheat germ in the blender till it's a fine powder. Mix with a half-cup of plain yogurt. Apply to face and allow to dry until the skin feels tight. Rinse off with warm water.

Or try 1 tablespoon of oatmeal mixed with eggwhite to remove dead skin and blackheads.

FACIAL MOISTURIZER

Clean face thoroughly. Wet your skin and apply a very small amount of petroleum jelly to it.

Continue wetting your face until the jelly is spread evenly and does not appear greasy.

FLY PREVENTION

Saturate a sponge with oil of lavender and place it in a shallow dish or pan. Put one in each room and pesky flies will disappear.

FOAM RUBBER, CUTTING

To get a straight, clean edge when cutting foam rubber, press a board with a straight edge into the foam as a cutting guide.

GIFT WRAPPING
Wrapping a piece of string around the gift makes a good guide for the length of paper needed to be cut.

GLASS, GLUE FOR
To attach objects to glass, melt together 1 part resin and 2 parts yellow wax.

GLASSES, FROSTY
For parties, fill glasses with hot water, pour it out and put them immediately in the freezer for 30 minutes or longer. This will keep them cold and frosty for serving.

GLUE, CAP FOR
Lost the glue cap? Use a suitably-sized nail. Or use a short length of candle instead. The glue also will not stick to the candle.

GLUE, DRIED
Add a few drops of glycerin to restore it to a usable condition.

GLUE, HOUSEHOLD
Add water to 1 cup of granulated laundry starch, till it reaches whipping cream consistency. Bring to a boil

and then allow to cool.

GLUE SPREADER

Plastic picnic forks hold a surprising amount of glue, and distribute it cleanly and smoothly.

GLUE STORAGE

To make sure the glue doesn't get dried up after it's been opened, make sure the cap is on tightly and then put the container in a large jar, and tightly cap it.

GLUE, STUCK LIDS

On a newly-opened jar of glue or paint, rub the threads inside the lid with a small amount of petroleum jelly. This will prevent the lid from sticking.

HAIR, CHEWING GUM IN

If a child gets chewing gum stuck in the hair, rub it with a little olive oil, witch hazel or peanut butter. Wash hair as normal after treatment.

HAIR, CUTTING

To cut bangs, comb them evenly over the forehead and place a strip of adhesive tape where you want to cut.

CUT HERE   TAPE

With scissors, cut across the top of the tape to get an even cut. This also prevents the cut hair from getting in eyes or over the floor.

HAIR, WASHING

To remove soapy film and get your hair shiny, put lemon juice (for blondes) or apple cider vinegar (for brunettes and redheads) in the final rinse water. Brunettes can also try rinsing hair with coffee, but not rinsing it out.

INK, WHITE OR PASTEL

To make white or pastel ink for writing in photo

163

albums or scrapbooks, dissolve a pinch of gum arabic in 1 ounce of water, and then crush and blend in a half-stick of white or colored chalk.

JEWELRY BEADS, RESTRINGING

Dip the end of the string into clear nail polish and let it dry. The thread will be easier to pass through even small beads.

JEWELRY, CLEANING

Clean amber or pearl beads with a little olive oil on a piece of flannel or chamois.

Soak rhinestone costume jewelry in detergent for 10 minutes and rub with a flannel cloth.

If metal jewelry gets dull, dunk in a small glass of detergent and water for a few minutes.

Wash pearls in warm soap water, rinse and lay them on tissue to dry. Do not rub them with anything except soft flannel or a dry chamois.

JEWELRY, RESETTING

If stones fall out of earrings or other costume jewelry, reset them with clear nail polish. Brush into the setting, press in your jewel and allow to dry thoroughly. If any polish pushes up around the stone, clean it off with cleansing tissue slightly dampened with nail polish remover.

JEWELRY, SKIN DISCOLORATION DUE TO
If costume jewelry leaves discolorations on your skin, try coating the contacting surfaces of the jewelry with colorless fingernail polish.

JEWELRY, TIGHT RING
If you cannot remove your ring, hold your hand in ice-cold soapsuds for a minute or so.

LABELING
Cut your name and address from the phone book to tape onto items such as glasses, pens, etc. In this way they can be more easily returned if lost.

To prevent smearing the address label on a package when sticking it on, roll a round pencil over it with your palm. Air bubbles will be released and the label will lay flat and smooth, and won't come off.

LEATHER, MILDEWED
Wipe with a cloth wrung out in a solution of equal parts of denatured alcohol and water. Dry in the open air. Or wash with the thick suds of a mild, neutral soap, rinse with a damp cloth and dry in an airy place.

LEATHER, RESTORATION
Rub the leather with the cut side of half a raw

potato, then polish.

LEATHER, SCUFFED

Trim off the scuffed flaps with scissors or a razor blade. Rub the rest of the scuffed area with your palm, brush on liquid stain polish and buff. Then apply paste polish.

LIPSTICK

Broken lipstick can be mended by softening the ends in a match flame, pressing them together and placing the lipstick in the fridge to harden.

LUGGAGE PROTECTION

Cover suitcases and bags with heavy garbage can liners and seal with adhesive tape. This will keep your luggage free from damage and dampness.

MATCHES, WATERPROOF

Dip ordinary matches into clear nail polish. Allow the nail polish to cover about half the match stick. It will also make them burn better in strong breezes.

MEASURE

Forgot your tape or ruler? Dollar bills are close to

6 inches long and 2.5 inches wide. 2 bills = 1 foot; bill folded in half = 3 inches or 1.5 inches.

MOVING
Pack a few of the most often used foods and spices in a medium size carton when moving. In your new location, they will be easier to find than hunting through containers where larger amounts of the supplies are packed.

NAIL POLISH, STUCK CAP
If the cap gets stuck, run it under hot water, which should loosen the polish.

To prevent the cap sticking, apply a little cold cream to the outside rim of the bottle when it's newly opened.

NEEDLE THREADING
To help thread a needle with heavy yarn, strip the paper from a wire tie used on bread wrappers or produce bags. Form the wire into a hairpin shape and use just like the smaller, commercial needle threaders. Or cut the thread at an angle.

NEWSPAPER CLIPPING, PRESERVATION
To preserve a newspaper clipping so it doesn't go

yellow or tear easily, dissolve a milk of magnesia tablet in a quart of club soda overnight. Pour the mixture into a pan large enough to accommodate the flattened newspaper clipping, and soak it for one hour, remove and gently pat dry. Do not move the clipping until it's completely dry. The clipping should last for many, many years.

PACKING BOXES

To make boxes easier to carry, cut a "half moon" slot in each end with a razor blade, and bend the flap inwards. This makes convenient hand grips.

PHONE CALLS, LONG DISTANCE

Write down what you want to say on a long distance call in advance. It will save you time and money.

PHOTOGRAPH ALBUM
Store the negative to your picture behind the print in your photo album.

PHOTOGRAPHS, MAINTENANCE
If photos curl, run them against the curl through your typewriter roll (make sure it's clean first, or cover the photo with a clean sheet of paper).

PIN CUSHION
Use a balsa wood block as a pin cushion. A dab of rubber cement will hold it in place and it can be easily removed. Or cover a ball of steel wool tightly with a good, hard-surfaced material. Will also prevent pins from rusting.

PURSE, STRAW
To refurbish an old straw purse, spray it with black or bright-colored enamel and staple brightly-colored artificial flowers on it.

SEWING MACHINE, EASE OF USE
Slip a pillow case over the drop leaf of your

sewing machine to keep the material from sliding as you work.

Keep a small magnet handy to pick up needles, pins, snaps, etc.

SEWING MACHINE, NEEDLE MAINTENANCE

When your sewing machine needle gets dull, rub it several times on a piece of fine emery cloth.

This will put a sharp point on it again.

SHOES, MAINTENANCE

Pre-treat new shoes by sprinkling them with talcum powder before you wear them the first time. This will help them be more comfortable.

Also, before wearing them for the first time, polish them to prevent deep scratches.

Rub your leather shoes every few days with petroleum jelly.

This will make them wear much longer and require less polishing.

Sponge black suede shoes with black coffee.

Renew buckskin shoes by going over them with a medium grade of sandpaper.

SHOE POLISH

A powder puff is perfect for applying shoe polish, as polish goes on smoother.

SHOES, SCUFFED

After polishing the shoes well, apply several layers of shellac to improve the look of bad scuffs.

If shoes are black, apply a touch of India ink, and then polish.

SHOES, SOFTENER

To soften water-hardened leather shoes or boots, rub with kerosene.

Or rub a damp cloth in saddle soap and massage the leather vigorously. Rinse well with a water-dampened cloth and dry away from heat source. When dry, apply polish.

SHOES, TIGHT HEELS

Moisten the inside of the back of the shoe, where the binding is sewn. Then heat the handle of an old metal knife on the stove, and when it is hot, pick it up with a potholder and pass the hot handle back and forth over the moistened inside of the shoe. This should stretch it out.

SOAP, LEFTOVER

Instead of throwing out slivers of leftover soap, drop them in a squeeze bottle, add warm water, and use as a liquid soap, adding more soap slivers when suds get thin.

STAMPS, STUCK TOGETHER

Lay a piece of thin paper over the stamps and run a moderately hot iron over the paper. The stamps will come apart and the glue will still be usable.

STAPLING

To let you know when it's time to refill your stapler, put a dab of bright-colored nail polish near the end of each bar of staples.

THREAD HOLDER

To prevent thread on a spool from unraveling, slip a rubber band around the spool.

TYPEWRITER CLEANING

To clean the type on the typewriter, use fingernail polish remover. However, do not try this on a computer printer of any kind.

WATER, FOR STEAM IRONS, CAR BATTERIES, ETC.

Collect the water which drip from the drain of your small air conditioner for use in your iron, battery, etc. Because it has been condensed, it will be better for the

172

equipment.

YARN & CORD HOLDER

Place the ball of yarn or cord in an upside-down saucepan, and thread the cord through the hole in the handle.

YARN SAVER

Wind unraveled used yarn onto a wide board and dampen it with water. Let it dry on the board and it will come out straightened and as good as new.

PAINT & VARNISH

BRUSH BRISTLES, LOOSE

Loose bristles can leave a jagged edge. Use an ordinary pocket comb to remove the loose bristles, and then rinse the comb in thinner.

BRUSH EXTENSION

To paint those hard to reach places in corners or under shelves, nail a small synthetic sponge to a yard stick or lath.

BRUSH MAINTENANCE

After cleaning your brushes with solvent and washing them with soap and water, clamp the bristles in a large spring clamp to keep them in shape, and hang on a hook till dry.

BRUSH RESTORATION

Soak hard, dry paint brushes in warm water with a small amount of lye in it. They'll come out soft and clean.

BRUSH STORAGE, TEMPORARY

Temporarily, a plastic bag will store a wet paintbrush without the paint on it hardening. Immerse the bag in water to exhaust the air from it and tie tightly.

BRUSH STORAGE

After thoroughly cleaning the brush, rub it with petroleum jelly and put in a dust-free storage place.

BRUSH WIPER

If you wrap a heavy rubber band lengthwise around the paint can, you can use it as an edge to wipe excess paint off the brush. The can will remain clean for resealing.

CAN HANDLES

Take the wire handle off the paint can. Take a wire clothes hanger and bend it as shown, and insert the ends in the bail holes. You can then hang the can on a nail, hook, tree limb or ladder rung.

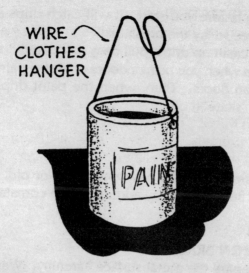

WIRE CLOTHES HANGER

PAIN

CELLAR STEPS

Paint your bottom cellar step with fluorescent paint to prevent accidents and to guide you when the cellar is dark.

DOOR PAINTING

To keep paint off hinges and other hardware when painting woodwork, coat them lightly with petroleum jelly. Any paint that does get on them will wipe off easily after the rest of the paint has dried.

DRIPS

For prevention, fasten a paper plate to the bottom

of the can before you start. It will catch drips and be a handy place to lay the brush.

To clean up drips, pull on a pair of old socks over your shoes when you paint indoors or where paint can be dripped on floors. Then, when the paint drips on the floor, just "skate" it off.

ENAMEL

When applying new enamel over old, you can prevent it from running by adding a little cornstarch to it.

ENAMEL ON BRASS

Prepare the metal surface carefully. Wash it well with any household cleaner that does not contain soap, then wipe it down with denatured alcohol. This will ensure the enamel will stick.

EYEGLASS PROTECTION

When you're painting, protect your eyeglasses from spatters by covering them with clear plastic kitchen wrap.

FLAKING

If new paint flakes off the wall, it may be because there are too many coats of old paint underneath. It's best to remove all old layers of paint, down to the plaster, and start from scratch.

FLOWER POTS, PAINTING

Place the flower pots upside down on a tin can. You can then reach all surfaces of the pot without soiling your hands.

TIN CAN

Or knot a rope through the drain hole, leaving the knot inside. Suspend the pot upside down to paint it, and allow to dry before removing the rope.

FRAME PAINTING

To paint a small picture frame without getting yourself and the frame messy, nail a thin wood strip to the back of the frame as a "handle" to use while painting. Remove it when paint is dry.

GOLD PAINT

All metallic gold paints eventually tarnish, since they are made from bronze powders rather than real gold. This can be prevented or postponed by giving the surface a coat of clear fresh shellac.

HANDS, PAINT ON

Rub hands with a small amount of cooking oil before washing them. It works wonders and the oil won't dry or roughen your skin as turpentine does.

LID OPENER

Drill a small hole in a short section of broomstick and drive in a large sheet metal screw almost all the way in. To open the can lid, place the edge of the screw under the lid and pry it off.

METAL, PAINTING

Paint applied to ordinary galvanized metal will usually peel off if the metal hasn't been pre-treated. Sponge metal with ordinary vinegar, let it stand for about one hour and then rinse off with plain water. Dry thoroughly before applying the paint.

MILDEW PREVENTION

Mildew can discolor paint.

Clean the area with a detergent or solution of trisodium phosphate. Rinse thoroughly and make sure the surface is completely dry before painting.

Repaint with a mildew-resistant paint, based on zinc oxide or similar.

Anti-mildew preparations are also available.

MIXING

Mixing paint is much easier if, for a few days prior to your paint job, you keep the paint can inverted so it will require less stirring. Or, pour it from one can to another, then back again. It will speed mixing and make sure the pigment blends completely with the oil.

ODOR PREVENTION

Add about 1 ounce of vanilla to each half gallon of paint and stir well.

ODOR REMOVAL

To get rid of the paint smell in a freshly painted room, cut a large onion in half, or put a teaspoon of ordinary household ammonia into a pan of water, and leave it in the room overnight.

PAINT BUCKET

For small painting jobs, pour the required amount

of paint into a coffee can equipped with a coat hanger wire handle. Run the wire though the holes in the sides of the can, with a loop on top to hold, and use it as a wiper for the brush.

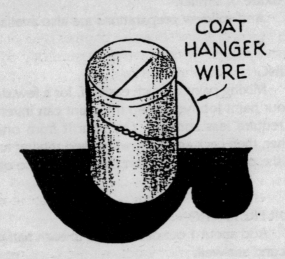

COAT
HANGER
WIRE

PAINT CADDY
There will be less mess and less chance of spillage if you organize all you need in a small, cut-off carton. Keep the paint can in the carton during use.

PAINT RECONDITIONING
If paint has become dry and apparently useless, try renovating it by pouring an inch of turpentine or mineral spirits on top, and letting it remain for a few days.

Stir well with a stick until it is soft and ready for practical use.

SHELLAC

Clear shellac is very versatile, but never use it outdoors as a primer under varnish or other clear finish or as a finish by itself. It turns white very quickly when it comes into contact with moisture.

SPATTER REMOVAL

To remove paint spatters from tile or linoleum, put a little dab of nail polish remover on a soft cloth and rub the spots.

To remove spatters from brick, use paint-remover and then wash with water.

If the paint is old, scrape off as much as possible with a putty knife and steel wool and use paint remover if necessary.

STAINS

To apply oil stains or water stains on raw wood, use a cellulose sponge instead of a brush for easier regulation of the amount being applied.

STORAGE

To keep a small amount of paint for future use,

pour enough hot paraffin wax on it to cover the surface. Then put the cover on the can. The paraffin will keep the air from the paint so it will stay fresh for a long time.

Or put a teaspoonful of turpentine in the bottom of a glass jar, put the paint can inside and seal it tightly, to saturate the air inside the jar and keep the paint from hardening. Add more turpentine after each use.

THINNER

To thin enamel, use clear varnish instead of paint thinner. This makes the enamel more durable and will not affect the color.

UNDERCOAT

If you want to paint dark interior woodwork white, first put on a coat of aluminum paint. Then only one coat of white paint or enamel will cover it.

VARNISHING

Put the can of varnish in a shallow pan of hot water. This will make the varnish flow easier and help it dry faster.

VARNISH REMOVER

Scrub old varnish from furniture or woodwork with a stiff-bristled brush and a strong, hot solution of washing soda. The loose varnish can be wiped off with old rags, without the usual gummy mess or odor.

WINDOW FRAMES

To paint window frames or screen frames, hold a piece of metal slat from a discarded venetian blind over the adjacent area of the screen or the glass to protect it from your paint brush.

To make sure the putty stays anchored to the glass, paint over the putty at least 1 eighth of an inch onto the glass. This will also prevent moisture from creeping in behind the putty and rotting your window sash.

PETS

BAD BREATH

   Clean the pet's teeth with dry baking soda on a piece of gauze.

BATHING, DOG

   If you bathe your dog in the bathtub, put a piece of steel wool over the drain hole so that the fur doesn't plug up the drain.

STEEL
WOOL

CARPET SOILING

   Blot up as much moisture as possible and rub the spot with a solution of vinegar or lemon juice and warm, sudsy water. Blot repeatedly. Then pour straight club soda over the spot and blot again. Place a dry towel over the stain and put a heavy weight (such as a book) on top of it.

When dried, dampen the spot with ammonia. This will not only take offensive odor away, but also prevent the animal from ever soiling that spot of the carpet again.

DISCIPLINE

If your pet keeps tearing up mats, rugs or other furnishings, try sprinkling cayenne pepper very lightly on the article. It should get rid of the habit.

FISHBOWL DECORATION

Use split shot sinkers as anchors for aquatic plants. This will stop them floating up. Just slip 1-2 small sinkers over each plant stem and crimp shut.

A few drops of food coloring in the water will make the bowl look more attractive and should not harm the fish.

FLEAS

Pine needles in the pet's bedding should keep him/her free of fleas.

FOOD FOR DOGS

Mix the water from cooking vegetables with the

dog food for extra vitamins and minerals.

LITTER BOX ODOR
Cover the bottom of the box with 1 part baking soda and then cover it with 3 parts litter.

MEDICATING CATS
Having trouble getting your cat to take liquid medicine? Put it on her fur, and she'll lick it off.

PLANT PROTECTION
Tired of the dog digging up your new plants? Stamp a few moth balls into the surrounding ground.

SCRATCHING POST FOR CATS
Cover a piece of scrap lumber with old carpet and rub it with catnip.

SHEDDING, DOGS
Massage olive, coconut or lanolin oil into his coat every 10 days or so. Feeding him 3 egg yolks each week will also give him a healthier coat. Also, try gently hand-vacuuming him frequently, unless he's scared of the machine.

SHEDDING ON UPHOLSTERY
Wipe the upholstery with a damp chamois.

SKUNK
Wash your dog or cat thoroughly in equal amounts of vinegar and water if he got too close to a skunk. Rinse with clear water, and repeat the vinegar and water treatment (weaker this time), but don't rinse it off.

TOYS FOR PUPPIES
Take a cleaned plastic bottle with a screw cap and put a few puppy biscuits inside it so it will rattle when shaken or tossed.

This will help stop him chewing other things.

WATER PAN, NON-TIP
So your pet doesn't spill his or her drinking water in the yard, drive a round stake in the ground and use a one-piece angel food cake pan as the water pan. Slide it over the stake.

STAKE

SAFETY & FIRST AID

BILL SPINDLES

If you have a sharp spike for putting paid bills on, bend the end into a hook to avoid spearing your hand.

BURGLAR-PROOFING

A good way to burglar-proof your valuables is to engrave your driver's license number on a non-removable part. Most thieves won't touch an item marked like this, and if it does get stolen and sold, the police can identify the owner in a matter of minutes.

CHILD LOCATION

If you have a small child wandering around your house, tie a small bell to his/her belt or shoe. This way you can hear where your child is. When the bell isn't ringing you know it's time to check and see what he/she is up to.

ELECTROCUTION

Always keep the number of your local fire department or rescue agency near the phones. Call them immediately.

If the patient is still in contact with the electrical source, try to break the contact without endangering yourself. Either pull the plug or hit a switch or turn the electricity off at the main switch box. Or, carefully, move the person away from the source with a nonconducting object such as a dry wooden stick or a rope.

Give artificial respiration if the patient's heart has stopped or if he/she has turned blue around the lips and face. Watch for signs of traumatic shock.

EMERGENCIES

Always keep emergency numbers near all the phones in your house so you don't have to run around in a panic trying to find the right number. The list should contain not only numbers for doctor, hospital, person to contact in emergencies, fire department number, etc., but also medical insurance policy number and brief details of vaccinations, illnesses and allergies, and household insurance policy number and contact.

Make sure your windows and screen doors can easily act as emergency exits.

FEET, ACHING
Soak aching feet in 2 cups of salt in a basin of hot water.

FIRE EXTINGUISHERS
Did you know that the wrong kind of fire extinguisher could make a fire worse?

The safest for all purposes is the general purpose, chemical, fire extinguisher.

FIRE PREVENTION
Make sure your furnace is clean of lint and dust, is well ventilated and that the pilot safety valve is working correctly.

Never put furniture close to a fireplace or heater.

Use a good smoke detector, and make sure it is run on batteries, or has a battery back-up. Replace batteries every 3 months. Electrically-run only smoke alarms will not work if there is an electrical fire.

Make sure your wiring is not worn and is sufficient for the number of appliances you use.

Don't pull the cord to get a plug out of the wall

socket.

Too many plugs and adapters in one outlet can cause a fire.

GAS LEAKS

Natural gas can cause explosions and fire.

If you smell gas in your home, get yourself and your family and pets out immediately. Call the gas company from a neighbor's house and let them know it's an emergency and to come out immediately.

Do nothing in your house that might cause a spark. This includes turning lights and appliances on or off, ringing the electric bell, using the phone and smoking.

When the gas company arrives, follow their directions implicitly.

Leaks can be found by lathering the pipe with soapy water. The escaping gas causes the soapy water to bubble. A temporary plug can be make by moistening a cake of soap and pressing it over the spot. When the soap hardens it should close the leak long enough to last until the gas man arrives. However, please also follow the above safety instructions for you and your family.

GLASS, BROKEN

Light bulbs: if the bulb has broken off in the socket, turn the light off first, take a cake of soap and press it over the broken ends and turn. Modeling clay or putty, or a bottle cork, can also be used.

On the floor: swab the area with wet, absorbent cotton. The tiny pieces of glass will stick to the cotton.

GLASS, SHIPPING

To send articles in glass containers, put the glass jars in tin cases from which the lids have been removed. Stuff paper around the jar and push the lid down. Wrap and mail!

HICCOUGHS

Try drinking a teaspoonful of granulated sugar mixed with vinegar. Repeat if necessary.

KNEE CUSHION

Take an old hot water bottle and stuff it with discarded stockings or foam pellets. Cork it up and use it for any job where you have to kneel. It's also easy to clean.

LYE

If lye is spilled on hands or clothing, wash with cold water immediately.

If it gets into the eyes, flush with cold water and call the doctor or emergency facility.

MATCHES, LENGTHENING

If the matches are too small to safely light candles or the fire in your fireplace, take an ordinary waxed paper drinking straw and use it as a taper.

MEDICINE, TO TAKE

Bad-tasting medicine tastes less bad if you de-sensitize your taste buds by holding an ice cube on your tongue for a few minutes before taking the medication.

PARTY DECORATIONS

Paper is very flammable. To protect your family and your house, use this recipe to make Christmas and party decorations flame retardant:

Dissolve 1 cup ammonia sulphate (buy at your local nursery), 6 tablespoons boric acid (available at your drug store), and 4 tablespoons borax (sold in your grocery store) in 3 cups of water. Put the mixture in a spray bottle. Spray all surfaces of the paper with a heavy mist, without saturating colored paper so it runs or stains. Allow a little time for the mixture to dry on the paper.

PESTICIDES

Always follow the directions on the label exactly. Be careful not to contaminate water, food, dishes, kitchens or utensils used by people or pets. Keep sprays away from open flames or electrical sparks. Wear gloves, as some pesticides can be absorbed through the skin.

Be careful not to inhale insecticide sprays and keep pets and children out of a treated room.

If you do get pesticides on the skin, wash all exposed areas with soap and warm water.

Dispose of the container in such a way that no one's small child can get hold of it. Instead of putting it directly in your trash can, keep it in a sealed container until trash day and see that it is carried away.

PILL TAKING, CHILDREN

If a child has trouble swallowing a pill, place it in a teaspoon of applesauce.

Remember to keep all medications out of the reach of children.

POISON

A "universal antidote" which works when you don't know which poison has been swallowed is:

2 parts powdered charcoal
1 part tannic acid
1 part magnesium oxide

Keep this mixture well mixed and in your medical cabinet for emergencies. Charcoal absorbs strychnine and phenol; tannic acid works with alkaloids, certain glucosides and many metals; magnesium oxide neutralizes acids.

Call your doctor immediately and keep the

patient warm. Try to dilute the poison with water or milk but only if the patient is conscious. Never induce vomiting.

POISON STORAGE

Keep all inflammable liquids, such as solvents, fuels, gasoline, etc., in metal cans with non-leaking tops. Do not use glass as the liquids may expand and burst the container.

ROOFS

When repairing your roof, don't stand. Move around on your hands and knees and have a safety line attached to a secure object such as the chimney or the top of the roof peak.

Don't leave your tools where you can step on them. Instead, keep them in a non-sliding tray above you.

Make sure your ladder is firmly secured at the base and firmly placed at the top.

SOLVENTS

All solvents, such as dry cleaning chemicals, etc., are very poisonous and also flammable. Store them out of the reach of children in tightly capped unbreakable containers, safely away from sparks or flames.

Solvent fumes are poisonous to breathe and the

solvent itself is poisonous if it comes in contact with the skin. Always work in a well-ventilated room, don't lean over your work, and use the solvent sparingly.

Make sure that children and pets aren't in the room when you're working so the solvent won't be spilled or drunk by your pet.

If you do spill the solvent, wash it off immediately. If any gets on your clothes, change them immediately and hang the clothing outdoors until the solvent has evaporated.

SORE THROATS

If your child has a sore throat, use a penny candy sucker as a tongue depressor to check it.

SPLINTERS, FINDING

Very small wood splinters in the flesh are difficult to see. Put a drop of iodine on the spot to make the splinter visible. Then remove with tweezers.

SPLINTERS, REMOVAL

Apply an ice cube to the area for several minutes to numb it. Dry thoroughly.

Cover the area with clear model glue (as used with model planes and other toys). When the glue is dry, peel it off with tweezers and the splinter will generally pull out with it. Repeat if necessary.

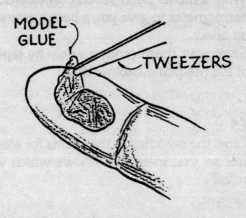

MODEL GLUE

TWEEZERS

Or soak the injured part in any cooking oil for a few minutes, to make the splinter easier to remove with tweezers

STEPLADDER

Paint the steps of the ladder and while the paint is still tacky, sprinkle coarse sand over them. After the paint has dried the steps will have a rough finish which will prevent slipping.

STEPS

To prevent accidents, paint the bottom step of the cellar stairs with reflective paint.

THERMOMETER

Wrap a rubber band several times around the end of the thermometer to give you a better grip so it doesn't drop and break.

Store your thermometer safely by taping it to the inside of the medicine cabinet door.

UTILITIES

Label the switches at the mains for electricity, gas and water so that everyone knows which way to turn them for "off".

WARNING LIGHT FOR CAR

Keep a few red balloons in your glove compartment with your flashlight. If you have a nighttime emergency, slip a balloon over the lens of your flashlight and it can act as a temporary warning signal. It also prevent rain getting in the flashlight.

RED BALLOON

WINDOWS & DOORS

BLINDS, BAMBOO, CLEANING
To clean bamboo blinds, use a strong solution of salt water. It will also help the blinds retain their natural shape.

BLINDS, BAMBOO, MILDEW PREVENTION
Paint a thin coat of clear shellac on the blinds.

BLINDS, CORD MAINTENANCE
To prevent knots on the ends of the blinds cords from untying, dip them in shellac while they are still tight. Let the knot soak up all the shellac it can absorb and allow to dry for a half-hour before using.

BLINDS, VENETIAN, CLEANING
Use a pair of mitts made from an old Turkish towel to speed up cleaning. Mitts can be made by outlining your hand on a sheet of paper and using it as a template.

Cut 4 sets, about an inch larger than your hand all the way around, from the towel, sew each 2 together and turn inside out. You'll be able to wipe both sides of each slat at the same time.

BLINDS, PULL IDENTIFICATION

Paint the "open" blind pull red with fingernail polish to save guesswork when you are in a hurry.

COAT HOOKS ON DOORS

If the door panel is thin, or is a cored-style door, use a sheet metal screw threaded all the way to its head to fasten a coat hook onto the door. Punch the starting hole with a heavy brad awl and tighten the screw only until it makes firm contact, or you might strip the threads.

CURTAIN ROD, BROKEN

When a sliding type curtain rod splits, a temporary repair can be made with a length of coat hanger wire. Bend the wire into a "hairpin" shape about 15 inches long, and spring it into the slots.

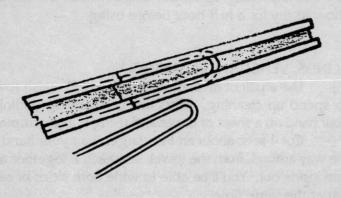

DOOR, TIGHT

Do you have a door that sticks when it is shut? To find out where exactly it's sticking, use a piece of carbon paper. Move it around the door jamb, opening and closing the door as you go. Smudges on the door show which spots need to be sanded.

Tape a strip of medium sandpaper at the area where the door binds on the frame. The action of opening and closing the door will soon smooth off the high spots.

Or give the edges a good coat of paste wax.

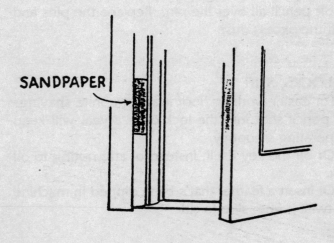

SANDPAPER

DOOR HINGES, SAGGING

When doors sag due to loose hinge screws, remove screws and fill the worn holes with twisted steel wool. Replace the screws; they will hold for a long time.

DOOR HINGES, SQUEAKY

A door hinge that persists in squeaking even though oiled, because the oil does not penetrate the full length of the pin, can be permanently silenced as follows: remove the hinge pin and rub the length of it with emery cloth to remove the rust, then file a flat surface the full length of the pin. Coat the pin with petroleum jelly and replace it in the hinge. The flat surface stores the lubricant and keeps the hinge quiet.

Interior doors that squeal and squeak can be quieted easily. Lift the hinge pins out, one at a time, and rub a soft pencil all over the pin. Replace the pins and wipe off the excess dust.

DOOR LOCKS, STIFF

For easier working door locks, graphite shavings from a pencil shot into the lock once a year will keep them operating smoothly.

Or oil the key itself, instead of attempting to oil the lock.

Or insert a feather that's been dipped in machine oil and twist it from side to side.

DOOR STOPS

For holding doors open, use plastic jugs filled with sand or dirt. Be sure to tape the jugs closed after they are filled. They can be quite ornamental if painted in bright colors or decorated.

If the door opens against something where you cannot use an regular door stop, cut about 1 third off a hollow rubber ball and slip the larger portion over the door knob.

DOOR, WARPED

Warped doors can often be straightened out by applying heat from an ordinary heat lamp to the convex side. Don't hold the lamp too closely, or the surface finish will get scorched. As soon as the warp disappears remove the heat. Then immediately coat both sides and edges of the door with sealer to prevent the re-entry of moisture.

DRAPES, CLEANING

To check whether sheer drapes need laundering, crush several folds together and hold up to the light. The dirt particles will stand out more clearly when bright light filters through the fabric folds than they would do through a single layer.

To launder them, add a tablespoon of powdered borax to the final rinse water. It will make them whiter.

DRAPE CORDS

To make the cords which operate your drapes work more smoothly, coat them with a thin layer of petroleum jelly.

FRAMES, ALUMINUM

To preserve the bright finish on aluminum door and window frames, coat them annually with silicone, available at auto supply stores. If you wipe some of the silicone into the window channels, the windows will slide more easily in cold weather.

Or prevent them from pitting by wiping them twice yearly with a cloth dipped in kerosene.

GLASS CLEANING

Never wash windows on sunny days as they will dry too fast and show streaks. Never use soap.

Always use up/down strokes to clean one side of glass, and left/right strokes to clean the other side. That way you'll know which side the streak is on.

Save old, stale liquid tea in a bottle and use for cleaning windows, mirrors, etc. Does a great job!

Or mix 1 half cup of ammonia with 1 half cup of white vinegar and 2 tablespoons of cornstarch in a bucket of warm water.

GLASS, CRACKED

A temporary hold for a cracked window is to hold it together with a coat of fresh white shellac. This won't obscure your vision, but will keep the weather out.

GLASS REPLACEMENT

To loosen a piece of window glass, pass a red hot poker slowly over the old putty.

To replace a piece of glass, take a piece of the old, broken glass with you to the glazier, so he can match it.

MOSQUITO REPELLENT

Cleaning door and window screens with kerosene will not only remove dust from the screen but stop mosquitos from settling on them.

SCREENS, SMALL HOLES IN

For small holes less than a half inch across, try using dabs of clear nail polish. Repeat after each coat dries until the hole is covered.

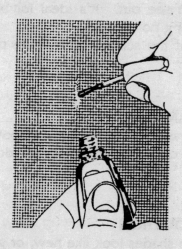

Or try filling in the gap with model airplane cement or similar.

SCREENS, PATCHING

To patch larger holes, cut rectangular pieces of scrap screen wire to the proper size, and fray the edges back a quarter inch or so. Bend the frayed wires over at right angles and work them through the spaces in your screen. To hold the patch in place, tap the bent-over edges with a hammer against a wooden block.

SCREENS, PRIVACY

To ensure privacy, paint your screens with aluminum paint. People won't be able to see in and you will be able to see out. It's ideal for bathrooms or screened sleeping porches.

Or, paint the screens with white paint thinned with turpentine.

SHADES, CLEANING

A soft eraser will remove many spots and stains. A rough flannel cloth dipped in flour will do an effective job on the dirt.

SHADES, RENOVATION

To make shades look like new, or give them an

207

interesting pattern or color, simple cover them with wallpaper.

SHADES, BLOWING

If your window shades blow about when they're down but the window is open, try replacing the ring on the string with a small suction cup, which can be stuck to the window sill to anchor the shade.

WINDOW FOGGING

If your windows fog up on the inside, usually it means the window isn't tight in the frame. Replace the window or install a soft clear plastic insert to create a double-paned effect. This will also help you save energy.

If the window is double-glazed, fogging is a sign of a broken seal and the window usually will have to be replaced.

Or, after the glass is thoroughly clean, rub it with a thin film of glycerin.

WINDOW, RATTLING

Inspect the window first to see what's making it rattle. If it's a loose pane or a loose sash in the frame, it can be temporary fixed by inserting a piece of cardboard, rubber or wood in the sash.

If it's the frame itself, it will need either filling or replacing.

YARDS, GARDENS & PATIOS

ANT EXTERMINATION

Place a flower pot upside down over the ant hill or nest and pour a teaspoonful of carbon tetrachloride through the hole. The fumes will sink and surround the ant hill, shutting out all oxygen. Or add clear water to used coffee grounds and pour the mixture over the nests. Repeat.

To prevent ants climbing the legs of your outdoor furniture, set the legs in caster cups filled with insecticide.

BARBECUE, CLEANING

Coat the bottom of skillets and other utensils with liquid detergent, to make them easier to clean afterwards.

BARBECUE TOOLS, CLEANING

Scrub them with a small brush sprinkling with washing soda.

BIRD FEEDER

Drill several large holes in different places in a log. Make up your own mixture of bird seed and bacon grease and pour into the holes. They'll love it!

BIRD SCARER

To stop birds using your home as a roosting place, and making a mess, fasten toy rubber or plastic snakes in the roosting places.

BRASS, CORROSION

Door knobs and other ornamental hardware can be protected from corrosion and pitting by periodically rubbing on a thin coating of paste wax. Clean the article first with metal polish or scouring powder. Rub was on and buff vigorously when dry.

BRICKS, PAINT REMOVAL FROM

To remove fresh paint from bricks, use paint remover and then wash with water. For old paint, scrape off as much as possible with a putty knife and steel wool, and then, if necessary, use paint remover.

BUG REPELLENT

General: plant nasturtium seeds. Bugs hate the peppery scent. Also, spray regular soapsuds on the plants.

Ants: pour boiling water on ant hills and nests.

Japanese beetles, carrot flies, aphids: plant onions and garlic near carrots, beets, lettuce and beans.

Roaches: don't like chrysanthemums. Save the blooms and let them dry. Shred them a little and scatter them in storage places, garages and behind stationary appliances, etc.

Worms and flies: plant basil near tomato plants.

CAST IRON, PITTED

Clean out the pits with steel wool and then smooth plastic steel over the article.

CHRISTMAS LIGHTS, OUTDOOR

To make small Christmas light bulbs appear larger, use aluminum foil (used is okay) as reflectors.

CLIMBING PLANTS

Ivy and other climbing plants can be persuaded to climb if you place the tendrils in the grooves between the bricks and plaster them into place with mud. By the time the mud falls away, the plant will have taken root.

COMPOST

It's great to add nutrients to the soil. Leaves, coffee grounds, tea leaves, glass clippings and kitchen scraps make good compost and add humus. Do not use meat or fat scraps. Turn over and mix once a week and keep it damp at all times.

CUSHIONS, FOR PATIO

Save old blankets and comforters, cut out the good parts, fold to cushion size and cover them with serviceable material.

FERTILIZER APPLICATION

Use an old funnel to apply fertilizer to individual plants. By covering the spout with your finger, you can dispense the right amount where needed.

FIREPLACE, OUTDOOR

An old oven rack or refrigerator shelf makes a

great grill for the outdoor fireplace.

FIREPLACE, OUTDOOR LIGHTING
Wrap ordinary kitchen matches in scraps of yarn and dip them in melted paraffin wax. Let them dry.

To strike, chip off the hardened paraffin from the tip end. They burn with intense heat.

FLOWER BOX MAINTENANCE
Cover the soil with a half-inch layer of gravel to prevent the soil from splashing when watered and stop it from drying out too quickly.

FLOWER BOX PRESERVATION
Whitewash the inside before you put in the soil and plants. It will control insects and preserve the wood.

GARDEN TOOL CLEANING
Scrape the mud off your tools with a scraper made from a piece of wood with bottle caps nailed to it.

GARDEN TOOL MAINTENANCE
When you put the tools away for the winter, jab them into clean, dry sand for storage to prevent rust and corrosion.

213

HAND CLEANING

After yard work, to get your hands and nails clean, scrub them with a damp nail brush sprinkled with dry baking soda.

HOSE COUPLINGS

So you don't lose the rubber washers for hose couplings, slip a small supply of them over a large nail driven into the wall near where you store your hose. Drive the nail at a slight downward angle so the washers won't slide off.

HOSE HOLDER

Wrap the hose under the handle of the pail and over the top before putting the end into the pail to fill it. It will stay in place. Take the hose out before shutting off the water to prevent water system back-up.

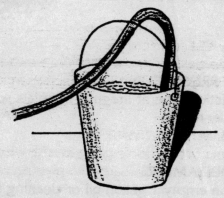

HOSE REPAIR
Apply one coat of pliable roof paint to seal leaks.

HOSE STORAGE
To prevent the hose from kinking, coil it in a figure 8, fold the loops together and hang it up. Uncoil to the figure 8 when using it again.

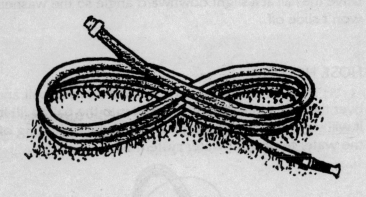

HOSE THEFT PREVENTION
Put friction tape at irregular intervals so it looks like it's a leaky hose.

LAWN & SOD TAMPER
Take an empty 1 gallon oil or cleaning fluid can,

cut a hole in the center of one side, to take a 5-foot length of 1-inch pipe. Screw a T joint to the pipe on the inside of the can, fill it with concrete mix and let it dry.

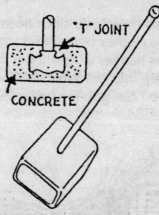

LITTER REMOVAL

A stick with a nail on the end picks up messy litter great. Carry a cardboard carton with a V notch cut in one side to scrape the litter off the nail. Litter goes straight into the carton.

MOLE REMOVAL

Sprinkle a few drops of castor oil or a few castor beans into the burrows. They hate it!

PANELING, OUTDOOR

Buy plywood or hardboard that is designed for exposure to the weather. Exterior plywood is glued with

216

waterproof glue.

PICNIC CLOTH

To prevent the picnic cloth from blowing away, clip a spring-type clothes pin on each corner, then push a wire pin (clothes hanger wire will do) through the hole in the spring deep into the ground. Bend the wire at a sharp angle so you can grip it when pulling it out.

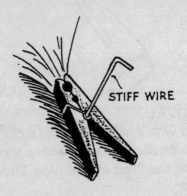

STIFF WIRE

PLANTING TO ENSURE HOUSE VENTILATION

Do not have dense shrubbery or other planting close to basement or house walls, as it prevent good ventilation and will increase humidity in the house.

PLANT PROTECTION

To protect tender plants from frost and other damage, cut the bottoms and tops off plastic jugs and place over the plants. Fasten plastic bags with a rubber band over the top. Hill the dirt around the bottom.

PLANT STAKES

Use small diameter extension curtain rods as stakes. As the plant grows you just pull up the extension end.

Or use an old piece of iron pipe or other hollow tubing. Water and plant food solutions can be poured into the pipe directly onto the roots of the plant.

PLASTIC FURNITURE, CLEANING

Dust the furniture regularly. Wipe with a damp cloth. Wash with lukewarm water and mild detergent. Do not use chemical cleaners such as ammonia.

POISON IVY AND OAK

To clear poison ivy or oak from your yard, spray with a solution of 1 gallon of soapy water and 3 pounds of salt. Repeat.

POTTING

Ordinary bottle caps with crimped edges are great in the bottom of clay flower pots to prevent loss of soil and water. Place one over the hole in the bottom of the pot before filling it with dirt.

RUST PREVENTION

To prevent rusting on bolts, dip the bolt threads in shellac and fasten nuts in position before the shellac has dried. Nuts will remove easily later.

RUST-PROOFING METAL

Buy a good grade of synthetic resin and mix with lamp black. Apply 2 heavy coats to any metal surface exposed to the weather.

RUST ON SIDING

May be caused by exposed nail heads corroding beneath the surface of the paint. Sand off the nail head and spot-prime with shellac or metal primer. Countersink the nail head and fill the hole with putty before repainting.

RUST ON STEEL

Cover the spot with sweet oil, rubbing in thoroughly, and let stand for a few days. Then rub briskly with powdered unslaked lime till the spots vanish.

RUST ON GARDEN TOOLS

Dip a soap-filled steel wool pad in kerosene or turpentine and scrub the tools. When most of the rust is gone, wad a piece of aluminum foil and rub the tool briskly.

SEED PLANTING

Put small seeds into an old salt shaker and sprinkle them lightly over the prepared soil.

SEED TESTING

To check old seeds are still alive, take a few from each packet and lay them between damp blotters (separate one for each seed packet).

If the seeds don't sprout in a few days, the other seeds in the packet are also no good.

SEEDLINGS

Plastic egg cartons make great planters to start seeds in the house before transplanting outside. Lift seedlings from the egg carton with a spoon.

SOIL, TO MAKE MORE ACIDIC

Sprinkle dried coffee grounds on the soil.

SNOW, SHOVELING

To prevent snow from sticking to the shovel, wax it with automobile wax.

TABLE, OUTDOOR

Weight down your tablecloth by inserting dowel rods in the hems so it won't blow away.

TIE-UPS FOR PLANTS

Cut the large plastic bags from the dry cleaners into to 2-inch wide strips for tie-ups.

Or, cut up old pantyhose.

TOMATO PLANTS, STARTING

Mix fireplace ashes into the surrounding soil. Remove the top and bottom lids from coffee cans and set a can over each plant, setting it firmly into the soil. Remove cans when plants are a few weeks old.

WEED KILLER

Dandelions: Put a drop of sulfuric acid into the heart of the flower or plant. Use a medicine dropper and be very careful the acid doesn't touch your skin. Keep out of reach of children and pets.

Grass: try salted boiling water, or just sprinkle salt.

WINDOW BOXES

To prevent the soil spattering rain onto your windows, put a layer of gravel on the top of the soil.